ICE CREAM COOKBOOK

SALT & STRAW

ICE CREAM COOKBOOK

TYLER MALEK

and JJ Goode

CLARKSON POTTER/PUBLISHERS
NEW YORK

CONTENTS

THE STORY OF SALT & STRAW

(AND WHY THIS BOOK EXISTS)

To understand Salt & Straw, you have to understand how we solved the Case of the Missing Caramel.

Portland, Oregon, 2011. It was a cold and rainy day, or it *probably* was because, well, we were in Portland. My cousin Kim and I had recently launched our pint-size ice cream business, selling scoops from a rickety cart with an erratic freezer. Kim handled the business. I made the product.

I had a vision of a flavor that riffed on salted caramel, infusing the *cream*, instead of the caramel, with salt. I made the ice cream, concocted a tasty caramel, and ribboned it into a three-gallon tub of the slightly saline ice cream so every scoop would have those irresistible streaks of burnt sugar. I was so proud. I put that first batch into the freezer to harden, opened it up the next day, and scooped out a serving. No caramel. That's funny, I thought, so I scooped. And scooped and scooped. Still no caramel. I stopped

scooping and made another batch, waited until the next day, scooped again, and still nothing!

Maybe I should mention that while my official Salt & Straw title at the time was Head Ice Cream Maker, it could also have been Only Ice Cream Maker. I was sort of like my own apprentice, messing up as often as I succeeded and learning something new with every churn. My inexperience did, however, give me one major advantage: Because I didn't yet know what I didn't know, I was daring. Before I'd successfully made vanilla ice cream, I had experimented swapping bone marrow for milk fat. I tried cold-steeping different varieties of tree barks in milk. I essentially home-brewed beers for the sole purpose of spinning them into ice cream. Whatever the flavor I dreamt up, I loved putting my lat-

est liquid concoction in the machine, pressing the button, and crossing my fingers. I ate both the successes and the failures—gleaning something from each one. Still, I couldn't serve salt ice cream with caramel without, you know, caramel. I had to get to the bottom of the mystery. I finally borrowed a hacksaw, cut the cardboard tub in half, and found it—a two-quart, golden brown pool at the bottom.

Fortunately I knew someone who could help: David Briggs. An early Salt & Straw customer, he also happens to be one of the best candy makers in the country and the chocolatier behind Portland's Xocolatl de David. He is creative, fearless, and wise—the man who merged Nutella with foie gras, who spiked his Valentine's Day chocolate hearts with pig's blood, and who out-Snickers-ed the Snickers bar, reimagining it with pecans and bacon-infused caramel. In other words, he was just the person who could help me solve my caramel crisis.

To my delight, David had taken to coming to hang in my kitchen almost daily after he finished up in his. We discussed the day's triumphs and flops. We brainstormed ridiculous flavors (sourdough ice cream!), which we sometimes made into reality (one day I did indeed churn a sludge of wild yeasts). When I mentioned my caramel problem, David didn't just help me troubleshoot—he gave me a master class on caramel. First, I learned the Why: The salt in the ice cream mixture slowed its freezing, giving the caramel time to sink to the bottom. Then I learned the What to Do:

I had to control the viscosity of the caramel. He showed me how to cook out the right amount of water by bringing the sugar and cream in the caramel to just the right temperature, which we ultimately determined to be 230°F. Not only did the caramel stay in elegant golden-brown streaks throughout the stark white ice cream, but it also had an almost magical texture—frozen but somehow still fluid, not sticking to your teeth but melting over them.

Now we had the perfect caramel and a delicious slightly salty ice cream. Or at least I thought it was delicious. Mark Bitterman disagreed. The author of the definitive book on salt and owner of a salt-focused shop (yes, really) in Portland, Mark came to Salt & Straw, tasted the ice cream, and asked to speak to me. When I met him, he had a briefcase and a stern look, like a CIA agent. Then the interrogation began.

"Did you use kosher salt to make this ice cream?" he asked with a furrowed brow.

"Uh, yes."

"I thought so," he said. Then the CIA agent became a character in *Harry Potter*. He clicked open his briefcase and revealed a hundred little vials tucked away in the briefcase's various secret compartments, hidden cubbies, and pop-up shelves. Each vial contained salt crystals in various shapes, colors, and sizes. For the next hour, I tasted them all, mixed with milk and cream, as Mark patiently schooled me on their finer points. By the end he had convinced me that he was passionate,

not scary, and that while kosher salt might work as steak seasoning, it wasn't right for this ice cream. Ultimately I fell in love with a Guatemalan *fleur de sel* that, he explained, had a particularly low minerality—it almost didn't taste salty. And once I had made and tasted a new batch of the ice cream, I became a convert. The salt brought out the nuances of the dairy, enhanced its natural sugars, and opened up my taste buds, welcoming the fat onto my tongue.

The creation of sea salt ice cream with caramel ribbons, now Salt & Straw's most popular flavor, was a turning point. It reflected everything I've come to love about Portland, where passion for food runs as high as generosity runs deep. They say it takes a village to raise a child. Well, we found out it takes a city to make an ice cream flavor.

Inspired by how much I learned from Briggs and Bitterman, I sought out collaboration. I found more mentors. I quizzed the best chocolatiers. I pestered my favorite chefs. I suited up in boots and an apron and joined the team at Breakside Brewery. After a crash course in malts and hops, we created an unfermented wort, a sort of pre-beer syrup, that was calibrated so that after undergoing the ice cream–making process (rather than the beer-making process), it would taste just like the ale it was meant to showcase. To accommodate all these projects, we decided that each month, our shops would not only offer an array of "classic" flavors—Arbequina olive oil, sea salt with caramel, cinnamon

snickerdoodle—but they'd also feature five new flavors with a shared theme—chocolate, beer, holidays, and many more. Then a month later, they would disappear, sometimes forever. Not only would this give customers yet another reason to return to our shop, but just as important, it would also force us to keep thinking, inventing, and meeting more and more people.

And all that, in short, is what this book is about. It's about our recipes, yes, so if you've had our ice creams and have a favorite scoop, you can make it at home. But it's also about that spirit of collaboration, learning, and experimentation. This book is meant to give you not just instructions, but also the insight into why these ideas work . . . and hopefully inspiration for you to take what's here and go make your own fantasy flavors a reality!

I might make the ice cream, but Salt & Straw wouldn't exist without my cousin Kim. She spent more than a decade working at Starbucks, starting out in the '90s when the company was just a regional coffee roaster with a few dozen stores, not the ubiquitous presence we all know now. Even way back then, she had toyed with the idea of opening an ice cream shop in Portland. Few things can compete with the pull of coffee—it's literally addictive!—but in ice cream, she saw the same potential for bringing people together. She envisioned a place where customers met the people who grew the strawberries or made the chocolate that went into their ice cream. She understood that, unlike coffee, you don't *need* ice cream, and that's how it derives its power. Because you don't need it, it feels special. Because it feels special, each lick brings with it pleasure and nostalgia and just plain eye-widening yumminess. If you're looking for a business that could inspire strangers to strike up a conversation about something they just tasted, you can do no better than ice cream.

But having a dream is the easy part. Back then, she couldn't quite summon the nerve to make it real. And as Starbucks boomed, she rose to, among other titles, Director of Frappuccino, so she put her dream on hold. When she finally left the corporate world at last to open an ice cream shop, the moment was right: The sense of community and genuine interaction she valued so highly was under assault by the iPhones and laptops that had come to define coffee shop culture. The only possible solution, *obviously,* was ice cream—it requires all of your attention, she'd say, because it melts!

When Kim called me, it wasn't to sell me on the idea of the shop—she just wanted to catch up—yet as I heard her plan, I couldn't fight the excitement I felt. When she mentioned that

her next step was finding someone to make the ice cream, I chimed in, "How about me?" "No way," she said. Her business, like most businesses, would probably fail. Family and business don't mix. Oh, and I had never made ice cream before.

I couldn't dispute the first two reasons, but I could do something about the last one. So an hour after we got off the phone, I walked into 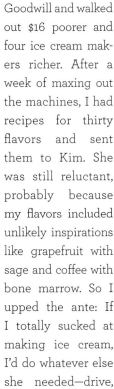 Goodwill and walked out $16 poorer and four ice cream makers richer. After a week of maxing out the machines, I had recipes for thirty flavors and sent them to Kim. She was still reluctant, probably because my flavors included unlikely inspirations like grapefruit with sage and coffee with bone marrow. So I upped the ante: If I totally sucked at making ice cream, I'd do whatever else she needed—drive, lug, organize, sweep—and for free. Finally she agreed to give me a shot.

I moved into Kim's basement in Portland and bought a stack of technical books on ice cream. Right away, the science captivated me. I couldn't stop reading about fat amalgamation and serum point equations. Soon I was tinkering with fat percentages and replacing milk and cream with olive oil and duck fat. I was experimenting with egg custards and xanthan gum and milk powder. When we were ready for our debut, we loaded up Kim's '76 Datsun (nicknamed The Red Donkey) with ice cream and drove to the annual Earth Day Clean Up on Alberta Street, where neighbors bonded over brooms, dustpans, and trash bags. For hours, we scooped out samples from buckets in the car's trunk. It was an amazing day. Even Fred Armisen and Carrie Brownstein came out to chip in! It was a very Portland beginning to a very Portland ice cream business.

About two years later, thanks to a bout of good press and an encouraging, supportive community, our business had taken off. We had three shops in Portland, just enough to keep us on the happy side of frantic. Yet whenever we traveled, inside and outside of Portland, we couldn't help wondering whether each neighborhood we liked would make a good place for another Salt & Straw.

While growing would benefit our amazing staff—if we didn't, there would be no way for employees to move up, so they end up moving on—we couldn't imagine a Salt & Straw clone in every town. After all, we made our ice creams in small batches. Our city—its farmers, artisans, nonprofits, and students—defined so many of our flavors. Ours was precisely the opposite of a business model built for expansion.

Yet, we thought, what if instead of cloning ourselves around the country, we started from scratch every time we entered a new community? Sure, it was exactly what the business books and gurus told you *not* to do. But if it worked for us, we would have created a new model, a way forward for businesses that wanted to grow without changing who they were.

In the spring of 2017, we got a huge boost of confidence in our risky idea when hospitality luminary and Shake Shack magnate Danny Meyer invested in our company. By the time this book hits shelves, we will have close to twenty-five shops in five cities. We've already opened locations in San Francisco, Seattle, and Los Angeles, each one thoroughly integrated into the fabric of the city. One day, I spotted proof on Instagram. A fan from L.A. had stumbled upon our original PDX location on Alberta Street. "Who knew?" she wrote. "There's a Salt & Straw in Portland, too!"

WHAT INSPIRES US

We called our operation Salt & Straw, a nod to ice cream history. Back in the day, there were no electric ice cream makers—just buckets of ice and salt. It was low tech and ingenious: Salt lowers the freezing point of water, which means that you can have a liquid colder than 32°F that you can then use to freeze other liquids. Insert a tub filled with sweetened cream into super-chilled water, use a crank to spin it and a paddle to scrape the edges, and soon you have ice cream, tubs of which were then packed in straw to keep the cold in.

Though our methods are a little more modern, we are inspired by ice cream's beginnings when it was a boundless vehicle for delight. Precursors to ice cream, in China and Persia, featured ingredients such as wine, quince, and camphor that might seem eye-rollingly modern by today's standards. When ice cream took root in France, you were just as likely to find frozen treats flavored with asparagus, artichokes, and fresh flowers as you were vanilla, then still an exotic import. In that light, our flavors, which tend to be viewed as avant-garde, actually harken back to an older way of making ice cream. Our parsnip and banana, India pale ale, and rose water flavors are fun, sure, yet in the history-long saga of ice cream, they're surely no stranger than freezer cases full of the same ten flavors.

One big reason why our flavors tend toward the unexpected is that I recognize that Salt & Straw, and most ice cream shops for that matter, face a nearly unbeatable competitor: nostalgia. That's why we've made more than five hundred flavors, including ice cream with actual blood and another with actual bugs, and a flavor called Berries, Barbecue, and Baked Beans (a bust, in case you were wondering!), but we've never made straight-up cookies and cream.

And while there's no actual straw at Salt & Straw, we have eschewed the industrial route in favor of relatively low-tech methods that let the imagination flourish. The big boys churn out 10,000 gallons of ice cream *every hour,* using massive machines that suck out train-car-size vats of cream and tanks of flavorings, spitting out runny ice cream that's shot through with chips or caramel and then flash-frozen. The person in charge can dial in the precise amount of air that he wants in the finished product. It's super cool. It's just not us.

We make ice cream in five-gallon batches. Our machines don't look much different from the typical 1½-quart home version. We flavor the cream, let the machine do its thing, then stir in mix-ins by hand. Our eyes, not a computer system, determine the right texture and the precise amount of mix-ins. And so we sacrifice efficiency and consistency for flexibility. Those sophisticated machines can't abide creativity, let alone the relentless invention that makes Salt & Straw what it is. Those fancy machines can't even, just to give one example, incorporate brownies that aren't rock-hard perfect squares! But we can, so we get to make the brownies slightly gooey so they'll still be yummy after they've been frozen. Our way, anything is possible. Whatever flavor we can imagine, whatever rule we want to break, and whatever we decide to mix in, we can figure out a way to accomplish it in our simple ice cream maker. And that means you can, too.

WITH   OREGON'S   BEST

CHOCOLATE with
GOOEY BROWNIES
ICE CREAM
made with
HOLY KAKOW

CINNAMON
SNICKERDOODLE
ICE CREAM
made with
RED APE CINNAMON

DOUBLE FOLD VANILLA
ICE CREAM
made with
SINGING DOG

HONEY LAVENDER
ICE CREAM
made with
BEE LOCAL HONEY

SEA SALT with
CARAMEL
RIBBONS
ICE CREAM
made with
THE MEADOW'S
FLEUR DE SEL

ICE CREAM
MONSTER MUGS

MAKING ICE CREAM IS FUN AND EASY, I SWEAR

(AND HERE'S WHY YOU'LL WANT TO MAKE OUR ICE CREAM)

Before I start rambling about butterfat percentages and ice crystal formation, before you dig into what might seem like ambitious recipes, I want to provide some reassurance: Making ice cream is not hard! While I want this book to inspire, to make you think and wonder, I also hope it just gets you *making ice cream*. Because making ice cream is plain fun.

This will be news to many people out there. Each of those ice cream machines I got at Goodwill when I was just starting out represents a person who once thought she would spend weekends churning away, only to give up before she got started. (Those poor machines looked pretty darn new, after all.) It's true, to those who have never done it, making ice cream can *seem* difficult or time-consuming. For this, I blame the product itself—the transformation of dairy and sugar to creamy perfection is so dramatic, so incredible, so much like magic, you could be forgiven for assuming that doing it yourself would require the same special skills, fuss, and labor that's necessary for macarons, croissants, and baguettes. The secret is that it doesn't.

We might be the people who brought you flavors like Bone Marrow & Bourbon Smoked Cherries, but you'll find no calls for Pacojets or canisters of liquid nitrogen here. All you need is a simple ice cream machine—no bells, whistles, or torque sensors required. It's what I used when I learned to make ice cream. And aside from a little extra horsepower to speed up the freezing process, it's essentially what we use at Salt & Straw today.

Here's another cool thing about the recipes in this book: Most of the ice creams use a base—a mixture they have in common—that requires *none* of the typical and precarious tempering of eggs. And better still, you can make the base in a big batch, keep it in the freezer, and thaw it when you're ready to flavor it with whatever you want and spin it into ice cream.

This, I hope, will make you even more likely to get ambitious and make bacon caramel and homemade peppermint patties. You might even find yourself sourcing Citra hops, floral liqueurs, and fresh huckleberries. Just as I like to think the scoops in our shops inspire conversations—strangers bonding over mutual enthusiasm for an unusual flavor or customers seeking out a beer after trying our frozen take—I hope this book does the same. I hope that when you serve Buttered Mashed Potatoes & Gravy ice cream, it gets

your friends talking and laughing and wondering. I hope that when you go to Dandelion Chocolate's San Francisco store—or its website—looking for nibs to make our cacao bean gelato, you end up buying a bag of unroasted beans and a few single-origin bars, just for fun. Or perhaps you'll look to your own city for great locally made chocolate or spirits or olive oil.

Maybe you'll treat this cookbook the way I do so many of my favorites—as a window into a chef's (or, okay, a harebrained ice cream maker's) creative process. By calling out little lessons embedded in the book's recipes, my goal was to create a book of ideas that can inform your own churning adventures. Following my recipes will guide you to my hard-won flavors, but carving your own path is not just okay but recommended. Because let's be honest, when you start with a good ingredient, add cream and sugar, then churn it, the result, no matter how badly you screw up the process, will taste pretty great. As long as it's frozen, it's going to be ice cream. And if it's not, pour it over a piece of cake—because, yum.

HOW ICE CREAM IS MADE, OR *THE MAGIC OF ICE CREAM*

Before we get into the particulars of making flavors like Caramel Corn on the Cob or Essence of Ghost, we should probably take a moment to ask, "What the heck *is* ice cream (and its family of supple frozen treats) anyway?" Well, everything from sorbet to ice cream begins as a tasty sweet liquid that's frozen in a machine. Some kind of machine is necessary because if you just put that liquid in the freezer, it would become a solid block of deliciousness—also known as a Popsicle. Whether the machine is crude or sophisticated, its purpose is to subject the sweet liquid to frigid temperatures while stirring it frequently, which means that you won't have one big block of ice, but a soft, scoopable mix of tiny, tiny ice crystals. Tada!

When a scoop really blows you away, it's because there was a little extra wisdom beyond the basic method. The good news is that this wisdom is built into the recipes in this book—you can make amazing ice cream without knowing any of the principles that make it so. Still, they're really neat, plus they'll guide you as you churn my creations

and maybe even your own. So let's take a trip inside the machine as the first step to explaining how ice cream is made, and how great ice cream is born.

Every home ice cream machine, no matter how fancy, is composed of a vessel, coolant, and a dull paddle known as a dasher. The vessel holds the tasty liquid. The coolant chills the vessel and thus the liquid. And the dasher spins around and around, powered by a motor or by a crank and some good old-fashioned arm strength. As the liquid makes contact with the super-cold vessel, the water in it freezes—that is, ice crystals form and grow against the walls of the vessel. Once those crystals reach a certain length, they're scraped from the walls by the dasher and folded back in until the liquid has become a collection of ice crystals. The ultimate size of these crystals is vital to the quality of your ice cream. If they're too large, they'd be noticeable on your tongue and will disrupt the smooth mouthfeel that marks a great scoop. If they're too small, they'll melt as they're folded back into the liquid and the mixture

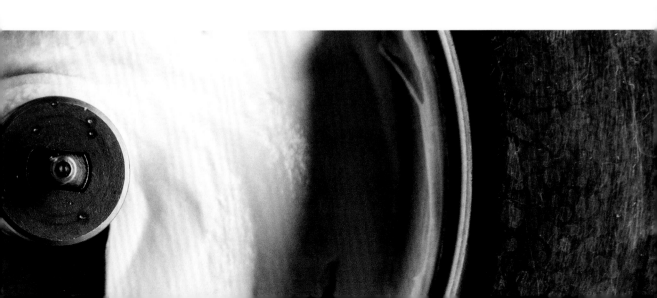

will never quite graduate from being a cold sweet liquid. What you want is lots and lots of tiny crystals, which add up to the almost silky quality of an awesome product.

Now for what goes into the machine: Let's start with sorbets. In sorbets, two of the main structural components—sugar and water—team up for a carefully choreographed dance. Aside from providing dopamine-inducing sweetness, sugar inhibits the freezing of water. When you use the right amount, that sugar keeps the ice crystals growing at just the right pace for the dasher to do its thing, and you get dense, velvety sorbet.

Sherbet, gelato, and ice cream are what you get when another partner joins the water and sugar on stage: butterfat. Like sugar, this fat affects both flavor and texture.

Fat effectively determines how you'll experience the flavor in each scoop. The higher the fat content, the more gradually you'll experience a flavor (say, strawberry) and the longer it'll last on your palate. That's why classic strawberry ice cream (lots of fat) evokes a mild strawberry-ness that lingers, while strawberry sorbet (zero fat) smacks you in the kisser with fresh fruit flavor, then vanishes. Fat affects texture because of the way fat changes in the machine. You know how furiously whisking heavy cream makes whipped cream? A sort of slow-motion version of this process happens when you make ice cream. As the machine spins, air gets trapped in the liquid, water forms ice crystals, and the fat transforms from separate itty-bitty droplets into a sort of web that includes ice and air. The practical result is the lush, creamy sensation and fluffiness that we associate with ice cream.

While most people don't think of air as a part of their ice cream, it affects how we experience a scoop. As a general rule, more fat means that by the time a mixture is done churning, your finished product will contain more air. Think about the fluffy quality of ice cream when compared with gelato, which has about half the fat and a texture that's about twice as dense, and sorbet, which has no fat and virtually no air and is as compact as can be. The lack of air affects flavor as well—after all, less air in each bite means more flavor in each bite.

Again, focusing on these particulars isn't necessary as you follow the recipes in this book. With the liquid mixtures calibrated just so, as they are in these recipes, the dance of ice cream making happens at just the right pace. The sugar slows down the freezing so that by the time the mixture reaches 23°F to 26°F, tiny ice crystals abound, the fat has had the chance to create its delicious web, and the optimal amount of air has been incorporated. Once you know a little about the role of these component parts, the method behind Salt & Straw's madness reveals itself, as we manipulate them to achieve the effect we envisioned.

FREEZING AND STORAGE:
ICE CREAM AFTER THE MACHINE

MIXING AND LAYERING

At our shops, we have a blast in our kitchens, catching ice cream as it flows from our machines in a bucket and spinning that bucket as we fastidiously drizzle in caramel or sprinkle in brownie chunks. Our goal is meticulously composed ice cream, precisely ninety scoops that have the same proportions—say, two nuggets of chocolate ganache, one and a half pieces of almond brittle, or three and a half streaks of caramel. This is the ice cream maker's equivalent of a chef plating a dish, when all the work of whittling vegetables, making sauces, and braising meat finally comes together. The hard work done, this part is pure fun!

Of course, the composition and those proportions are also totally subjective. So while each recipe in this book has carefully calibrated amounts of mix-ins and particular instructions for layering them with the ice cream, never forget that my goal for each scoop need not be yours. If you're big on chunks of cookies or prefer just a few thin streaks of caramel or think it'd be cool to have a thick layer of yummy jam in the middle of a pint, go for it!

FREEZE IT FAST

Now, you have reached an important moment in the life of your ice cream: The churning has stopped. The mixture resembles soft-serve in appearance. You can totally eat the ice cream now, and it'll be delicious! But you don't yet have the scoopable treat you're after. To get there, you have to bring the temperature down from 26°F–23°F all the way to 10°F–0°F, when it hardens into the ice cream we all know and love. Remember how I went on and on about how important it is that your frozen treat is a collection of many tiny ice crystals? Right after churning is the point at which it will have the greatest number of tiny crystals. Maintaining them during the hardening process is crucial. To do so, you have to get your ice cream as cold as possible, as quickly as possible.

Inevitably, you're going to lose some of those ice crystals—the tiniest ones in particular, which begin to melt when the ice cream comes out of the machine. You do, however, need to limit the loss and even more important, prevent the remaining ice crystals from *growing*. This happens when some crystals melt into water and then, during the hardening process, latch on to the remaining crystals, making them bigger. The bigger they are, the more you'll feel them in your mouth, weird and grainy, when you eat the ice cream; if you've ever tried to save a half-molten pint of ice cream by popping it in the freezer to refreeze, you know what I'm talking about. So how do you chill down ice cream at home effectively and how do you best keep it good and cold until you're ready to enjoy it?

- If your freezer gives you the ability to control the temperature, reduce it as much as you can a few hours before you make ice cream.
- Ideally, clear out a zone in the back of the freezer. It's the most consistently cold part of the freezer, far from the warm air that

rushes in when you open the door looking for ice cubes or leftover soup.

- Leave enough space in this zone to store the containers without other frozen miscellanea butting up against them. This maximizes the airflow around the container, and flowing cold air is what cools down the ice cream.
- And of course, when you transfer the ice cream from the machine to containers and the containers to the freezer, do it as quickly as you can.

KEEP IT COLD

The ice cream is frozen hard—you did it! At this point, ice cream has a single enemy: heat shock. This is the industry term for what happens when ice cream melts and then freezes again. The melting and refreezing might be microscopic, or it might be obvious. Maybe it's because the freezer door was open too long when you were deciding which frozen pizza to have. Maybe you were watching *Twin Peaks* on your couch with your arm around a pint but only finished half. Whatever the reason, you must avoid this at all costs. As we know, when melted ice crystals refreeze, they latch onto lingering crystals, giving you ice cream in which they are fewer and larger. The good news is we can help prevent heat shock.

In fact, there is a top-secret, foolproof way to treat ice cream so it stays at optimum deliciousness for its entire life: Eat it. Now. In one sitting. If you eat your freshly hardened ice cream now, it won't have a chance to experience the sorts of temperature spikes you get from opening and closing the freezer door. If you eat it in one sitting, it won't refreeze. Call it gluttony for the sake of ice cream perfection. If you don't yet possess such courage, fear not: A few simple measures can pretty much guarantee that you'll prevent heat shock.

1. Keep your ice cream in the back of the freezer.
2. Shield it from rushes of warm air in the freezer, building walls around it with packages of frozen fruit or vegetables, ice cube trays, or even pints of other ice cream that don't deserve protective measures.
3. Get an ice cream coozy. Seriously, these exist, at every level of nerdiness from the familiar foam sleeve to the hand-knit! Because the exterior of the ice cream is what's most affected by the warm air, insulating the sides of the container protects the most vulnerable ice crystals.

EQUIPMENT (AND ONE IMPORTANT INGREDIENT NOTE!)

Before you dig into the recipes, I want to provide a little guidance on the types of ice cream makers out there and the lowdown on their benefits and quirks. Because our ice creams often feature cookies, caramels, and other tasty mix-ins, you'll want to make sure you have a few other tools on hand as well.

THE THREE TYPES OF ICE CREAM MAKERS

Ice cream machines come in all shapes and sizes. There are fancy ones with bells and whistles and simple ones with . . . just bells. The options here all work well and differ mainly in the amount of planning, patience, and maintenance they require. I recommend a 1½-quart capacity machine for these recipes, though, as overloading a 1-quart machine can prevent your ice cream from freezing properly. At the end of the day, however, they're pretty much the same in that they can all produce delicious ice cream.

HAND-CRANK

These are a bit of a novelty in a modern market filled with electric machines, but I love the way they remind you of the early days of ice cream making. They rely on simple chemistry: A vessel containing the cream mixture sits in another full of ice and salt. The salt lowers the freezing point of the ice, creating a liquid with a temperature that's lower than 32°F to act as your chilling element. Instead of electric-powered churning, you turn the crank yourself. That's part of the fun (you get to participate in the churning!) and the fuss (you *have* to participate in the churning!). One cool benefit is that you can churn ice cream in less time than

you can with most electric machines. I hold the title of the fastest hand churner in Portland, thank you very much.

CHURNING TIME: *Hand-crank machines will generally turn your liquid mixture to ice cream in 5 to 15 minutes, depending on your arm strength.*

> ### COLD ~~HOT~~ TIP!
> *If you use a hand-crank device, try this: Rather than a mixture of ice and salt, use ice and an intense salt brine (a one-to-one salt-to-water ratio by volume). That gets things cooler quicker.*

FROZEN-BOWL

A common type of machine, this one churns with an electric motor; the chill is provided by a bowl filled with coolant that you must store in the freezer for 24 hours before using. (The freezable bowls with paddles are also sold as an attachment for stand mixers.) The downside is that between batches of ice cream, you have to freeze the bowl again for another 12 to 24 hours. If you have a crowded freezer or make ice cream more than once a day, that's a bummer. Another downside: Since the bowl has a finite amount of chilling power, you have to make sure everything—the ice cream base, the flavoring—is already very cold, which often means another few hours of fridge time.

The upside: If you're willing to make room and plan a day in advance, you'll get a great result, and these machines tend to be much more affordable than the ones with an internal compressor.

CHURNING TIME: *Frozen-bowl machines will generally turn your liquid mixture to ice cream in 20 to 30 minutes, provided that the mixture you use is already very cold from the fridge.*

> **TIP**
>
> *If you're using a frozen-bowl machine, thoroughly chill your base and flavorings. If your machine allows it, turn it on before adding the ice cream mixture. In the rare case that your machine is struggling to freeze the mixture, next time try churning half at a time.*

INTERNAL COMPRESSOR

These machines have compressors that create their own cold, the way your freezer does. The biggest upsides: You don't have to prefreeze a bowl before or between batches. And you can load these machines with cool, rather than super-cold, mixtures with barely any effect on quality. No more chilling a mixture for hours and hours before churning.

This is in the big-league category with prices to match: starting at $150 and going up according to size and compressor strength. A stronger compressor means quicker churning and quicker churning means less air, better butterfat structure, and better ice cream. Okay, *slightly* better ice cream. It's up to you whether the marginal difference in quality is worth the extra dough.

CHURNING TIME: *Most machines with an internal compressor will turn your liquid mixture to ice cream in 30 to 40 minutes. Super-fancy ones will take 12 to 18 minutes.*

CONTAINERS

To store your ice cream, you can use virtually any container you'd like. Round plastic pint or quart containers, like the kind your Chinese takeout or deli salads come in, and thick paper containers (sold with the descriptor "soup to go" at restaurant supply stores and online) are solid picks for home use—easily available, more or less airtight, and thin enough to encourage rapid hardening of the ice cream in your freezer. Metal containers are less common, but because metal conducts cold well, they will help freeze your ice cream quickly, as long as they're prefrozen. Glass is a no-no; it's prone to breaking at low temperatures.

Keep in mind that the ice cream at the center of the container, insulated from the cold by both the container itself and the ice cream around it, will be the last part to freeze and could suffer slightly as a result. For that reason, small containers are better than large containers. But the only real rule to how you fill the containers is that you should leave a little space (a half inch or so) at the top, because ice cream expands slightly as it freezes. (Don't worry about under-filling the containers—see "Parchment Paper," below.)

PARCHMENT PAPER

Because few container lids are actually airtight, I add an extra layer of protection. This prevents ice crystals from forming on the surface of the ice cream, a result of the relatively warm air outside of the freezer collecting beneath the lid, condensing into moisture, and freezing. (Note that this is totally different from the problem of ice crystals disappearing and growing *inside* the ice cream.) Still, it's annoying and who hasn't opened a pint to see the bummer of ice on the ice cream? One way to prevent this is to keep a piece of parchment paper pressed to the surface of the ice cream, just as you'd press plastic wrap against the top of pudding to prevent a skin from forming. Then cover the container with the lid, letting the parchment hang over the sides if necessary. Don't have parchment? Just close the lid, flip the container upside down, and freeze it like that.

STICK BLENDER

I recommend a stick blender (also intimidatingly called an immersion blender), especially for use at home. Not only do they take up less counter space, but they're great for blending relatively small home-batch-size mixtures, which may not work well in a full-size countertop blender.

SILICONE BAKING MATS

Whether you're baking cookies and pecan pie bars or making toffee, skip parchment paper or foil and buy a few silicone mats (often called by a common brand name, Silpats) to make your life easier and less messy.

CANDY THERMOMETER

Making certain candy confections, like fluffs and caramels, requires relatively precise temperature readings. So you'll need a thermometer that can register temperatures up to, oh, about 400°F. Spare yourself the waiting and the potential sugar-burning and go instant-

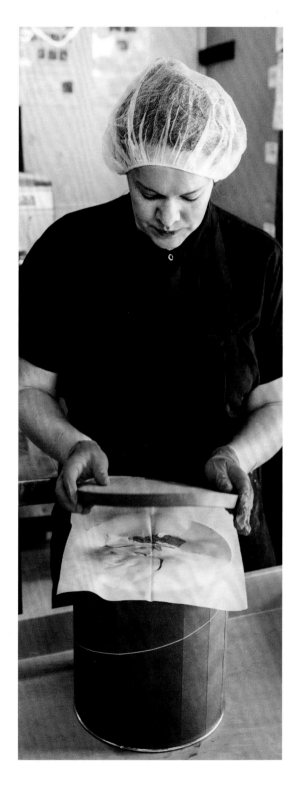

read digital, which will register the temperature in a matter of seconds.

ICE CREAM SCOOPS

You do not need a proper scoop to eat ice cream. I've successfully consumed mint chip, cookie dough, and rocky road with spoons, forks, spatulas, and butter knives. But I do love a good-looking scoop! Save those trigger scoops for dough and cafeteria-style potato salad. Use ice cream spades for shoveling (transferring from machine to containers), not scooping. Skip the scoops with pointed tips (they're unnecessary, even a little dangerous, if you ask me). And pay no mind to scoops with antifreeze inside. Unless you're scooping all day, there's no point. My home scoop of choice is a plain-old two-ounce standard scoop made by Zeroll. But you can still scoop like a pro.

1. **Dip the scoop in *cold* water.** A cold-water-dipped scoop will carve a path without melting the ice cream.

2. **Shake the scoop dry.** A totally dry scoop sticks to the ice cream. A wet scoop makes the orbs of ice cream weirdly glossy, not to mention it adds water where water is not welcome. A shaken-dry scoop gives you scoops with picture-perfect crevices.

3. **Lock your wrist.**

4. **Run the scoop along the ice cream's surface, starting at the far side and pulling it toward you.** (Do not shovel, dig, or um, scoop.) After two or three pulls, the scoop will curl the ice cream up into a nice tight ball and you'll have what you're after.

KOSHER SALT

Kosher salt is kosher salt, right? Not exactly. The same volume of kosher salt from the two most common brands, Diamond Crystal and Morton, will have a very different impact. Because of the size of the grains, a teaspoon of Morton contributes almost twice the saltiness of a teaspoon of Diamond. I vastly prefer cooking with Diamond—I like the way it feels between my fingers—so the amounts provided in this book are based on it. If you're using Morton, use about two-thirds as much as I call for.

CHAPTER 1

BASES

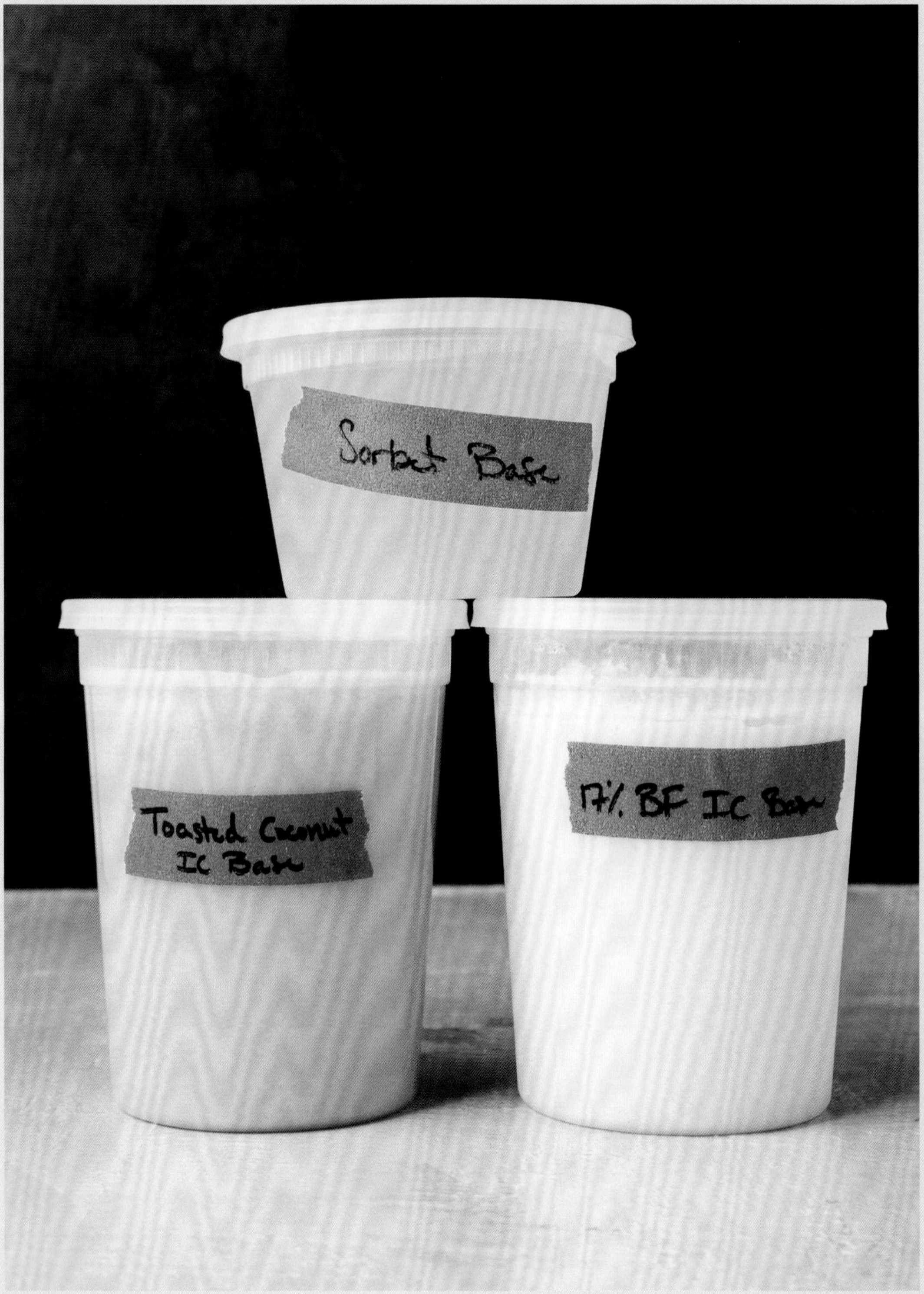
Sorbet Base
Toasted Coconut
IC Base
17% BF IC Base

My ice creams, sorbets, and everything in between start with what's called a base—the concoction that is to the frozen treats what stocks are to soups. You can flavor stock with carrots, celery, or onion (just the way you can flavor an ice cream base with chocolate, vanilla, or strawberry). Or you can *add to* the stock ingredients things like chunks of chicken and noodles (think chips, caramel, or cookie dough). Or you can do both— hello, seafood chowder; hi, mint chocolate chip! Whatever you decide to do, the base is your ice cream's jumping-off point.

In this chapter, you'll find the two bases that are used for just about every recipe in this book— one for ice cream and one for sorbet and gelato— plus an amazing vegan ice cream base. (Later on in the book, there are a few custard bases that are unique to their recipes.) All these bases are pretty darn simple. They don't require ice baths, instant-read thermometers, or precarious tempering of egg yolks. You mix, you heat, you stir, you're done. This is no concession to home cooks, either. It's exactly what we do at Salt & Straw.

BUT FIRST THE SECRET SUPERHERO OF ICE CREAM

So you've stored your ice cream just the way I told you to. You shoveled it from machine to container with haste. You've dutifully tucked it in the very back of the freezer and employed a phalanx of frozen expendables to defend it from the warm world beyond. Wait, what's that you say? You didn't?

Okay, I get it. Even at Salt & Straw, where we have a rigorous high-tech distribution system—store at –20°F, deliver at –10°F, temper in shop to –5°F, scoop at 5°F—the unexpected happens. We understand that we just can't manage every second of the ice cream's life. At home, you have more control but less fancy technology and, I assume, less will to focus all of your energies on maintaining the crystal structure of your ice cream. Who out there can save America's pints from an icy fate? Why, look! There, in the bag! It's flour, it's sugar, it's . . . xanthan gum!

Every recipe in this book uses xanthan gum in its base. Now, I know what you're thinking (it's exactly what I thought when I first heard of it): "Xanthan gum" sounds funny. It starts with an "x"! It must be impossible to find and it must be bad. Well, it's not and it's not! It's easy to get, not just online but at most supermarkets. It's sold by ubiquitous brands like Bob's Red Mill and Hodgson Mill. Second, although that "x" makes it sound especially unnatural, xanthan gum is no stranger than cornstarch or baking soda.

Xanthan gum has one vital purpose at Salt & Straw: We use it to combat heat shock. To think about how, consider the effect that the more familiar gelatin has on water. Like xanthan gum, gelatin is a hydrocolloid. And

as anyone who has made Jell-O knows, gelatin can halt the flow of water. While technically xanthan gum's actual effect on water is slightly different, the upshot is the same. It inhibits the mobility of the melted ice crystals (a.k.a. water) in ice cream, so the water has a harder time migrating to and refreezing onto those remaining crystals, making undesirable growth produced by heat shock less likely.

Some large companies use xanthan and other gums to mimic the texture of fat as well—so they can cut back on pricey cream—but the crutch comes with its own cost. Leaning too heavily on the stuff gives the product a gummy, teeth-coating texture that lingers on your palate a bit too long, like that guy at the party who hangs out after everyone else has gone home. Just the right amount of xanthan gum, on the other hand, is miraculous. At no cost to ice cream quality, you get insurance against ice crystal growth, bumpers in the bowling lane of perfection, a little leeway for when the world inevitably conspires against you. It's the lone ice cream–making decision at Salt & Straw that makes our lives easier, not harder. And being freed from that worry lets us be more daring on other fronts. My hope is that the freedom encourages you to make more ice cream!

And while most homemade ice creams are best eaten within a few days, xanthan gum is one of the reasons why the ice creams in this book keep for three months!

ICE CREAM BASE

MAKES ABOUT
3
CUPS

The perfect scoop of ice cream begins here. In minutes you have the foundation for practically every creamy frozen treat in this book—plus an infinite number you can create yourself. Make it, store it, flavor it, and churn away. That's all you *need* to know.

For the curious, however, there's more going on in each base than meets the eye. What might read like an arbitrary list of ingredients is in fact a formula that yields a carefully calibrated ratio of ice cream's main components. (For ice cream nerds, it's approximately 58% water, 17% fat, 11% milk solids, and 14% sugar, by weight.) That's not to say that a final product with these ratios is necessarily the goal. In some cases, I want an ice cream that has, say, a lower fat percentage—remember, less fat means a denser texture and flavor that hits your palate more quickly—so I might ultimately dilute the base when I add a flavoring before churning. For us at Salt & Straw, the base is the way we keep track of our starting point, which makes manipulating the finished product much easier.

For the home cook, carving out a separate recipe for the base has a different purpose. It's practical and makes home ice cream making that much easier: This way, you can make it in advance—in big storable batches, even—so each recipe in this book is that much easier to execute.

¹/2 cup granulated sugar

2 tablespoons dry milk powder

¹/4 teaspoon xanthan gum (Yes, I'm easy to find! See page 33.)

2 tablespoons light corn syrup

1¹/3 cups whole milk

1¹/3 cups heavy cream

Combine the sugar, dry milk, and xanthan gum in a small bowl and stir well.

Pour the corn syrup into a medium pot and stir in the whole milk. Add the sugar mixture and immediately whisk vigorously until smooth. Set the pot over medium heat and cook, stirring often and adjusting the heat if necessary to prevent a simmer, until the sugar has fully dissolved, about 3 minutes. Remove the pot from the heat.

Add the cream and whisk until fully combined. Transfer the mixture to an airtight container and refrigerate until well chilled, at least 6 hours, or for even better texture and flavor, 24 hours. Stir the base back together if it separates during the resting time. The base can be further stored in the fridge for up to 1 week or in the freezer for up to 3 months. (Just be sure to fully thaw the frozen base before using it.)

NOTE

Following the instructions for the bases will yield a few more tablespoons than the amount called for in the recipes. This is intentional—so you're sure to have enough base, even when a bit inevitably gets left behind here and there in the pan, in the storage container, and the like.

AN EVEN BETTER ICE CREAM BASE

In ice cream industry circles, we talk about "aging" a base. When you make this base and then stick it in the fridge overnight before freezing it, you give the proteins in the milk, which were stressed when heated, a chance to relax. No, it's not 100 percent necessary, but it's highly recommended. Your ice cream will be markedly better—the texture smoother, the milk flavor more robust—like the way stews taste better the day after you make them.

SORBET (OR GELATO) BASE

MAKES ABOUT
2
CUPS

This base is designed to make sorbet, gelato, and everything in between. For sorbets, you essentially just add flavor—say, a puree of roasted strawberries (see page 89) or even roasted banana and parsnips (see page 157). For the rest, you add flavor *and* fat—a little cream to reach sherbet status, or a bit more to achieve a gelato-grade treat.

1 cup granulated sugar

½ teaspoon xanthan gum (Yes, I'm easy to find! See page 33.)

¼ cup light corn syrup

Stir together the sugar and xanthan gum in a small bowl. Combine 1¼ cups water and the corn syrup in a small saucepan. Add the sugar mixture and immediately whisk vigorously until smooth (but don't fret over a few lumps). Set the pan over medium heat and cook, stirring often and adjusting the heat if necessary to prevent a simmer, until the sugar has fully dissolved, about 3 minutes. Take the pan off the heat and let the mixture cool completely.

Transfer the mixture to an airtight container and store in the fridge until cold, at least 4 hours, or up to 2 weeks, or in the freezer for up to 1 year. (Just be sure to fully thaw it and stir well before using it.)

COCONUT ICE CREAM BASE (DAIRY FREE!)

MAKES ABOUT

4

CUPS

Gregory Gourdet, the chef at Departure and a rockstar of Portland's food scene, turned us on to this incredible base for dairy-free ice cream. Coconut cream provides both fat and flavor, which is boosted by an infusion of the fruit's toasted shredded flesh.

$^1/_2$ cup unsweetened shredded coconut

$^1/_2$ cup (lightly packed) light brown sugar

$^1/_4$ cup granulated sugar

$^1/_2$ teaspoon xanthan gum (Yes, I'm easy to find! See page 33.)

$^3/_4$ cup light corn syrup

$2^1/_2$ cups unsweetened coconut cream (preferably Aroy-D and boxed, not canned)

Heat the oven to 300°F.

Sprinkle the shredded coconut in an even layer on a sheet pan and bake, shaking the pan occasionally, until the coconut is an even dark amber color, about 5 minutes.

Meanwhile, in a small bowl, stir together the brown sugar, granulated sugar, and xanthan gum.

Combine the toasted coconut, corn syrup, and 1 cup water in a small saucepan. Add the sugar mixture and whisk vigorously until smooth. Set the pan over medium heat and cook, stirring often and adjusting the heat if necessary to prevent a simmer, until the sugar has fully dissolved, about 3 minutes. Remove the pan from the heat and stir in the coconut cream.

Let the base cool. Transfer the mixture to an airtight container and refrigerate until well chilled, at least 6 hours, or for even better texture and flavor, 24 hours. The base can be further stored in the fridge for up to 2 weeks or in the freezer for up to 3 months. (Just be sure to fully thaw the frozen base before using it.) Strain it before using.

MAKE EXTRA!

Since I've never read an ice cream book that says this—and I've read a lot of ice cream books—let me take a moment to shout here: *There's no need to make a base every time you want to make ice cream.* Our base recipes can be doubled, tripled, and quadrupled without worry. Do it! They keep in the fridge for up to a week (2 for sorbet or coconut bases), or in the freezer for up to 3 months. Since you'll be using bases in 2-cup (for sorbets) or 3-cup (for ice creams) batches, consider freezing them in those size batches, too. That way, you just have to thaw them completely, flavor them as directed in each recipe, and churn fresh ice cream whenever you want! One note: After about 24 hours in the refrigerator, the base mixtures will likely separate. That's no problem—just stir them back together before using.

ICE CREAM BASE

2X / 6 CUPS
1 cup granulated sugar

1/4 cup dry milk powder

1/2 teaspoon xanthan gum

1/4 cup light corn syrup

2 2/3 cups whole milk

2 2/3 cups heavy cream

3X / 9 CUPS
1 1/2 cups granulated sugar

6 tablespoons dry milk powder

3/4 teaspoon xanthan gum

6 tablespoons light corn syrup

4 cups whole milk

4 cups heavy cream

4X / 12 CUPS
2 cups granulated sugar

1/2 cup dry milk powder

1 teaspoon xanthan gum

1/2 cup light corn syrup

5 1/3 cups whole milk

5 1/3 cups heavy cream

COCONUT ICE CREAM BASE

2X / 8 CUPS

1 cup unsweetened shredded coconut

1 cup (lightly packed) light brown sugar

$1/2$ cup granulated sugar

1 teaspoon xanthan gum

$1^1/2$ cups light corn syrup

2 cups water

5 cups unsweetened coconut cream (preferably Aroy-D and boxed, not canned)

3X / 12 CUPS

$1^1/2$ cups unsweetened shredded coconut

$1^1/2$ cups (lightly packed) light brown sugar

$3/4$ cup granulated sugar

$1^1/2$ teaspoons xanthan gum

$2^1/2$ cups light corn syrup

3 cups water

$7^1/2$ cups unsweetened coconut cream (preferably Aroy-D and boxed, not canned)

4X / 16 CUPS

2 cups unsweetened shredded coconut

2 cups (lightly packed) light brown sugar

1 cup granulated sugar

2 teaspoons xanthan gum

3 cups light corn syrup

4 cups water

10 cups unsweetened coconut cream (preferably Aroy-D and boxed, not canned)

SORBET (OR GELATO) BASE

2X / 4 CUPS

2 cups granulated sugar

1 teaspoon xanthan gum

$2^1/2$ cups water

$1/2$ cup light corn syrup

3X / 6 CUPS

3 cups granulated sugar

$1^1/2$ teaspoons xanthan gum

$3^3/4$ cups water

$3/4$ cup light corn syrup

4X / 8 CUPS

4 cups granulated sugar

2 teaspoons xanthan gum

5 cups water

1 cup light corn syrup

CHAPTER 2

SALT

& STRAW

CLASSICS

Each month, our shops feature a five-flavor deep-dive into some delicious subject—from Thanksgiving to chocolate, berries to beer. This monthly roster of special flavors gives customers an opportunity for exploration, and the promise of it causes me to keep thinking, inventing, and meeting more and more awesome people to inspire and teach me. But not everyone craving a cone wants an adventure. Sometimes you just want to enjoy your pet flavor for the fifth time in five days. That's where these fourteen classics come in, which—with a few city-specific variations— are available at Salt & Straw all the time.

And while the flavors are decidedly different from the standards of your average ice cream parlor—you know, chocolate, strawberry, rocky road, etc.—they do share the same purpose: Each one set outs to meet a fundamental desire. Just as rocky road satisfies fillings-lovers and chocolate pleases purists, our new classics fulfill the need-states of the modern ice cream enthusiast. For instance, to appease the sweet-salty obsessive, we have sea salt ice cream with caramel ribbons. To indulge the two main types of chocolate fanatic, we offer cocoa powder–powered ice cream with gooey brownies (for those after nostalgia) and bean-to-bar bliss (for those after a Third Wave experience). There's a flavor for the locavore adventurer (Oregon pear and blue cheese!), for the vegan who wants to join in the fun (made with coconut cream caramel and almond milk ganache!), and for the eight-year-old in all of us (hello, snickerdoodle!).

The only overlap is vanilla. Here we take a stand for the underappreciated ingredient, a magical seedpod whose flavor is one of the most complex on earth but, thanks to an epidemic of cheap extracts, has become a synonym for "dull." Our vanilla ice cream sets out to both satisfy and change minds.

ARBEQUINA OLIVE OIL

MAKES ABOUT

1½

PINTS

This is ambitious ice cream at its simplest. Because while it's as easy as whipping up a batch of vanilla, its flavor is unexpected (and incredibly delicious!) and the science behind two fats arranged in frozen marriage is super cool. The result is a perfect example of how ice cream can serve as a creamy platform to showcase an ingredient—in this case, great olive oil. (We use the glorious stuff made from Arbequina olives grown and pressed at Red Ridge Farm, in Oregon's Willamette Valley.) Each lick features the oil's round texture and its sweet, grassy, and almost tropical flavors, all guided onto your taste buds by rich, cozy butterfat.

WHAT WE LEARN: *You can play around with this recipe, swapping in your favorite olive oil, walnut oil (as we do at our L.A. stores, using the excellent La Nogalera), hazelnut oil, or really any oil that doesn't solidify at room temperature (I'm looking at you, coconut oil). For a real nerd alert, most ice cream contains just one type of fat—butterfat from the dairy. But in this case, the oil joins the fun. Technically, they don't actually combine, but because they're frozen, they hold together in a group hug, creating a lush texture halfway between creamy and silky. If you let the ice cream melt, you'd eventually see them separate.*

3 cups Ice Cream Base (page 34), very cold

¼ cup Red Ridge Farm Arbequina olive oil (order it online!) or another grassy olive oil

½ teaspoon kosher salt

Put the ice cream base, olive oil, and salt into a bowl and whisk until the oil is well dispersed; there will still be visible little droplets on the surface. Pour the mixture into an ice cream maker and turn on the machine. Churn just until the mixture has the texture of soft-serve (see pages 23 to 24 for timing ranges, depending on the machine).

Quickly transfer the ice cream, scraping every last delicious drop from the machine, into freezer-friendly containers. Cover with parchment paper, pressing it to the surface of the ice cream so it adheres, then cover with a lid. It's okay if the parchment hangs over the rim. Store it in the coldest part of your freezer (farthest from the door) until firm, at least 6 hours. It will keep for up to 3 months.

Arbequina Olive Oil Ice Cream

STUMPTOWN COFFEE & BURNSIDE BOURBON

MAKES ABOUT

2½

PINTS

Portland is a coffee town, so we couldn't make just *any* coffee ice cream; we designed one to show off top-quality beans. Chocolate enhances coffee's roasty, caramely qualities and a healthy dose of whiskey adds depth and a boozy wallop. Our original version of this ice cream features a trio of local legends: single-origin coffee from Stumptown, cocoa powder from Holy Kakow, and Eastside Distilling's exceptional barrel-aged Burnside bourbon. Not to worry, non-Portlanders: Any high-quality substitutes will work.

WHAT WE LEARN: *Alcohol (in the bourbon) plays a cool role in this recipe. Because it shares the freezing-depressant properties of sugar, the addition lets us dial down the sweetness of the cream without sacrificing the velvety consistency. And that allows the nuances of that great coffee to shine.*

1 cup coarsely ground coffee (see Note)

½ cup Burnside bourbon or your favorite bourbon

1 cup heavy cream

1 tablespoon granulated sugar

2 tablespoons unsweetened cocoa powder (preferably natural)

3 cups Ice Cream Base (page 34), very cold

Combine ¾ cup of the coffee grounds, ½ cup cold water, and the bourbon in a glass jar. Cover it tightly and shake lightly. Let it sit, covered, at room temperature for at least 24 hours (or up to 3 days with little impact on the flavor).

Using a fine-mesh strainer, strain the mixture into a container, pressing the grounds to extract as much liquid as you can. Discard the grounds. If you spot any stray coffee grounds in the mixture, strain it once more. Store it in a sealed container in the fridge for up to 2 weeks.

Combine the cream and sugar in a small saucepan and cook, stirring, over medium-high heat until the cream gives off steam but isn't yet bubbling, about 3 minutes. Reduce the heat to low, add the remaining ¼ cup coffee grounds and the cocoa powder, and whisk for a minute or so to dissolve the cocoa powder. Remove the pan from the heat and let the cream and coffee hang out together for 30 minutes, stirring occasionally to achieve maximum flavor extraction (a.k.a. coffee yumminess).

Pour the mixture through a fine-mesh strainer into a container, pressing the grounds to extract as much liquid as you can; then discard them. Let the coffee cream cool to room temperature, then stir in the cold brew–bourbon mixture. Transfer it to the fridge to chill until cold if you're using a pre-frozen bowl type of machine; otherwise, use it now or refrigerate it for up to 3 days.

Put the ice cream base and 1 cup of the coffee-cream mixture into a bowl and whisk to combine. Pour the mixture into an ice cream maker and turn on the machine. Churn just until it has the texture of soft-serve (see pages 23 to 24 for timing ranges, depending on the machine).

Quickly transfer the ice cream, scraping every last delicious drop from the machine, into freezer-friendly containers. Cover with parchment paper, pressing it to the surface of the ice cream so it adheres, then cover with a lid. It's okay if the parchment hangs over the rim. Store it in the coldest part of your freezer (farthest from the door) until firm, at least 6 hours. It will keep for up to 3 months.

NOTE

To make awesome coffee ice cream, you need awesome cold brew. So buy high-quality beans, freshly roasted. For this recipe, I like coffees that bring to mind stuff like tobacco, caramel, maple, and dark chocolate, so look out for beans like that. Grind the coffee beans coarsely but just a bit finer than you'd use for French press, or ask a barista to do it.

FRECKLED WOODBLOCK CHOCOLATE

MAKES ABOUT

2

PINTS

Woodblock Chocolate owners Jessica and Charley Wheelock were the first bean-to-bar makers in Portland. They do it all: sourcing cocoa beans from farms around the world, roasting them in a nineteenth-century fire roaster, grinding them, and making freak-out-worthy bars. Our goal was a flavor worthy of their craft. We make a simple chocolate ice cream, set off the chocolate with a little sea salt—we love Jacobsen, the first company to harvest salt from the Oregon coast since the era of Lewis and Clark—and stipple scoops with teeny, quick-melting chocolate chips that deliver an immediate rush of flavor.

WHAT WE LEARN: *The chocolate "chips" in these scoops are created by a cool, dead-simple technique called freckling, which can be applied to any ice cream, though it does require an ice cream machine with a chute or opening that lets you add ingredients while you're churning. Just pour melted chocolate, spiked with a little oil, into the ice cream right at the end of churning, with the machine still running. The melted chocolate hits the dasher and scatters into a million tiny bits. Not only do they look cool, but these freckles of chocolate are effectively untempered, so unlike typical chocolate chips that stay waxy and flavorless until they finally melt in your mouth, these liquefy the moment they hit your tongue.*

1¼ teaspoons Jacobsen Oregon-Harvested Salt or another flaky sea salt

2 tablespoons granulated sugar

5 ounces single-origin Woodblock Chocolate or another great dark chocolate, chopped into chip-size pieces

3 cups Ice Cream Base (page 34), very cold

1 teaspoon vegetable oil

In a medium (about 1½-quart) saucepan, heat ¼ cup water, the salt, and the sugar over medium-high heat until the water gives off steam but isn't yet bubbling, about 1 minute. Remove the pan from the heat, add 3 ounces (about ½ cup) of the chopped chocolate, and stir until the chocolate is completely melted. Let it cool to room temperature. Pour in the ice cream base, then use a whisk or stick blender to mix or blend until smooth. Chill in the fridge until cold if using a pre-frozen bowl machine.

Pour the mixture into an ice cream maker and churn just until it has the texture of soft-serve (see pages 23 to 24 for timing ranges, depending on the machine).

While the ice cream is churning, pour an inch or so of water into a small saucepan and bring it to a simmer over medium-high heat. Combine the remaining 2 ounces (about ⅓ cup) chocolate pieces and the vegetable oil in a heatproof bowl that'll sit on top of the saucepan without touching the water. Put the bowl over the saucepan, reduce the heat to low, and heat, stirring occasionally, until the chocolate is completely melted. Take the pan off the heat but leave the bowl on top. The chocolate will stay warm until the ice cream is churned.

Once the ice cream is churned to about soft-serve texture, lift the bowl of melted chocolate from the pan and dry the bottom of the bowl. With the machine still running, pour the melted chocolate through the chute in a very thin, steady stream. The warm chocolate will scatter and harden into freckles when it hits the cold ice cream.

Quickly transfer the ice cream, scraping every last delicious drop from the machine, into freezer-friendly containers. Cover with parchment paper, pressing it to the surface of the ice cream so it adheres, then cover with a lid. It's okay if the parchment hangs over the rim. Store it in the coldest part of your freezer (farthest from the door) until firm, at least 6 hours. It will keep for up to 3 months.

CHOCOLATE GOOEY BROWNIE

MAKES ABOUT
2½
PINTS

Our version of this modern classic combines super-delicious chocolate ice cream made with fair-trade Holy Kakow cocoa and brownies designed to stay ooey-gooey when frozen. Visitors to our kitchen will be hard-pressed not to spot the secret to our brownie magic: giant buckets of homemade marshmallow fluff!

¼ cup granulated sugar

¼ cup unsweetened natural cocoa powder, preferably from Holy Kakow

3 cups Ice Cream Base (page 34), very cold

1 cup Gooey Brownie pieces (recipe follows)

Combine the sugar and ¼ cup water in a small saucepan, set it over medium heat, and bring to a boil. Remove from the heat and whisk in the cocoa powder until the mixture is smooth and glossy, about 15 seconds. Let it cool to room temperature. Put the ice cream base and the chocolate mixture into a bowl and whisk to combine. Transfer it to the fridge to chill until cold if you're using a pre-frozen bowl type of machine.

Pour the mixture into an ice cream maker and turn on the machine. Churn just until it has the texture of soft-serve (see pages 23 to 24 for timing ranges, depending on the machine).

Quickly transfer the mixture to freezer-friendly containers: Spoon in a layer of ice cream, sprinkle on some brownies, and use a spoon to press them in gently. Repeat. Cover with parchment paper, pressing it to the surface of the ice cream so it adheres, then cover with a lid. It's okay if the parchment hangs over the rim. Store it in the coldest part of your freezer (farthest from the door) until firm, at least 6 hours. It will keep for up to 3 months.

GOOEY BROWNIES

MAKES ABOUT 5 CUPS OF BROWNIE PIECES

8 tablespoons
(1 stick) unsalted
butter, cut into
1-inch chunks

3/4 cup (5 ounces)
chocolate chips

2 large eggs

3/4 cup granulated
sugar

1/2 cup all-purpose
flour

1/4 cup unsweetened
cocoa powder (any
kind, but Dutch-
processed is
especially great
here)

2 teaspoons kosher
salt

1/2 cup heavy cream

1 cup marshmallow
fluff (store-bought
or make the Lemon
Marshmallow Fluff,
page 124, without
the lemon zest)

Homemade marshmallow fluff is the secret ingredient in our ice cream-friendly brownies. The addition prevents the brownies from soaking up cream (and getting icy when frozen), so they stay as gooey-soft in each scoop as a perfectly undercooked brownie is straight from the baking pan. They're so soft, it's best to store them in the freezer until you're ready to use them.

Heat the oven to 350°F. Line a 9 × 9-inch baking dish with parchment paper and spray it with nonstick spray.

Pour an inch or so of water into a small saucepan and bring it to a simmer. Put the butter in a heatproof bowl that'll sit on top of the saucepan without touching the water. Set the bowl on the saucepan, reduce the heat to low, and let the butter melt completely, stirring it occasionally. Add the chocolate chips and stir until the chocolate is completely melted. As soon as it's fully melted, remove the pan and bowl from the heat but keep the bowl over the warm water.

In a stand mixer fitted with the paddle attachment, beat the eggs and sugar until the eggs look lighter in color and slightly frothy, about 3 minutes. Reduce the speed to low, add the chocolate mixture to the eggs, then increase the speed to medium-high and mix until completely combined.

In a separate mixing bowl, lightly whisk together the flour, cocoa powder, and salt to break up any clumps. Turn off the stand mixer, add the flour mixture, and mix on medium speed until the ingredients are just combined. Reduce the mixer speed to low, slowly drizzle in the heavy cream, and continue to mix until just combined, scraping down the sides as necessary. Use a large spoon to fold the marshmallow fluff into the batter, mixing just enough to get most of the fluff incorporated with just a few streaks remaining.

Pour the batter into the prepared baking dish and spread it out to make an even layer. Bake until a butter knife inserted into the center comes out clean and the top is crackly but the brownies are sticky and ooey-gooey, about 30 minutes. Let them cool completely, then cut them into ½-inch pieces. Freeze them in sealed freezer bags until cold before using; they will keep for up to 2 months.

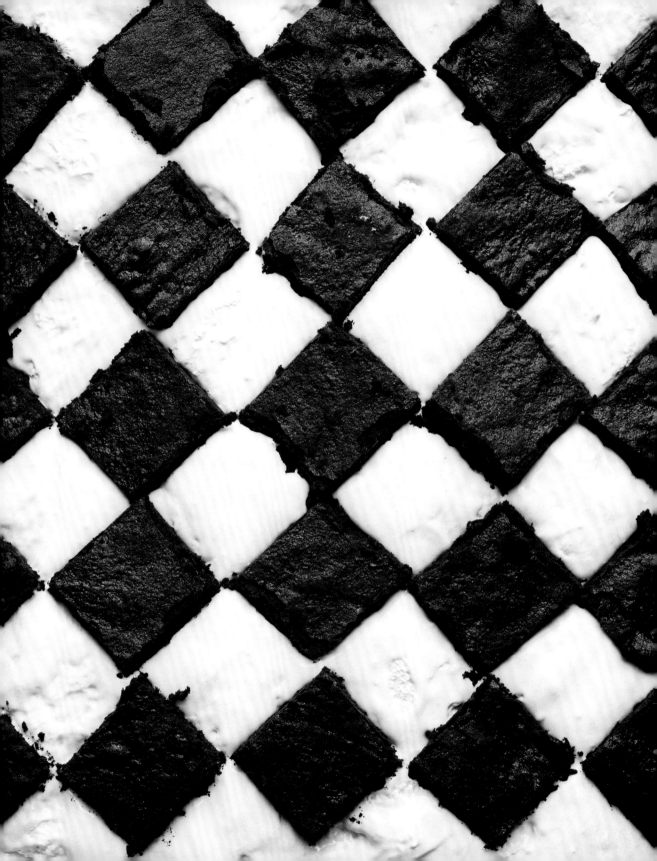

XOCOLATL DE DAVID'S BACON RALEIGH BAR

This flavor pays tribute to David Briggs, the candy wizard behind Xocolatl de David. A few months after he bigheartedly revolutionized my caramel making, I approached him with a crazy idea. I was in love with his Bacon Raleigh Bar. A mind-warping take on the Snickers bar, it's a miniature slab of pecan-spiked nougat topped with smoky bacon-infused caramel then dipped in fine chocolate. It's possibly the best chocolate bar on the planet. I wanted to make it into ice cream. Sure, I could have just taken his creation, chopped it up, and stirred it into vanilla ice cream, but the bar, designed to be eaten at room temperature, would be distorted beyond recognition by the freezing process. Instead, with David's help, I decided to take the bar apart, component by awesome component, and reengineer it in frozen form. The result is one of the more complicated recipes in the book, because it requires you to make three separate candy treats. Yet press on! Each one can be made well in advance and provides plenty extra for snacking.

WHAT WE LEARN: *Caramel made with cream is a joy for anyone who likes to experiment. Water and fat extract flavors differently. Because cream is composed of both water and fat, it gives you a chance to lock in the full flavor profile of an ingredient, and in this recipe, that means you get both bacon's round porky flavor, which latches onto the water, and its smoky, lardy qualities, which attach to the fat. But there's no reason to stop at bacon. Try infusing rose petals, basil leaves, toasted oats, and other yummy things. Once the infusing is done, the rest is caramel as usual.*

1¼ teaspoons fleur de sel

3 cups Ice Cream Base (page 34), very cold

½ cup chopped Chocolate-Covered Pecans (recipe follows)

½ cup Bacon Caramel (recipe follows)

½ cup Chocolate Nougat Crème (recipe follows)

Combine ¼ cup water and the fleur de sel in a small saucepan, set it over medium heat, and cook, stirring, just until the salt has completely dissolved, about 1 minute. Let it cool to room temperature.

Put the salt water and the ice cream base into a bowl and whisk to combine. Pour the mixture into an ice cream maker and turn on the machine. Churn just until the mixture has the texture of soft-serve (see pages 23 to 24 for timing ranges, depending on the machine).

(recipe continues)

Meanwhile, put the caramel in a warm place (such as near the stove) so it's drizzleable but not so warm that it'll melt the ice cream.

Quickly alternate spooning layers of the ice cream, a sprinkle of the chocolate-covered pecans, a generous drizzle of the bacon caramel, and dollops of the chocolate nougat crème in freezer-friendly containers.

Cover with parchment paper, pressing it to the surface of the ice cream so it adheres, then cover with a lid. It's okay if the parchment hangs over the rim. Store it in the coldest part of your freezer (farthest from the door) until firm, at least 6 hours. It will keep for up to 3 months.

CHOCOLATE-COVERED PECANS

MAKES ABOUT 1 CUP

1/3 cup chopped dark chocolate

2 tablespoons unsalted butter, cut into cubes

1/2 teaspoon fleur de sel

1 cup pecan halves

Sure, you could buy these, but melting chocolate with a little butter takes almost no effort—there's no shame in using a microwave—and tossing in the pecans is pure fun. A sprinkle of fancy salt makes them extra special.

If you are using a microwave, combine the chocolate, butter, and fleur de sel in a microwave-safe bowl and microwave on low, stirring occasionally, until fully melted. Or to use a double boiler, pour an inch or so of water into a small saucepan and bring it to a simmer. Combine the chocolate, butter, and fleur de sel in a heatproof bowl that'll sit on the saucepan without touching the water. Set the bowl on the pan and heat, stirring often, until fully melted.

Let the chocolate mixture cool until it's about body temperature. Add the pecans, and stir until the pecans are completely coated in chocolate. Pour the pecan mixture onto a parchment-lined sheet pan and cool (preferably in the freezer) until the chocolate hardens completely.

Chop the hardened chocolate-covered pecans into ¼- to ½-inch pieces. They can be used immediately or stored in the freezer for up to 6 months.

BACON CARAMEL

MAKES ABOUT 2 CUPS

4 thick slices
  bacon (preferably
  a high-quality,
  super-smoky one
  like Nueske's),
  coarsely chopped

1 cup heavy cream

1½ cups granulated
  sugar

¼ cup light corn
  syrup

3 tablespoons cold
  unsalted butter,
  cut into cubes

½ teaspoon kosher
  salt

Caramel is good. Bacon caramel is better.

In a small saucepan, heat the bacon over medium heat until it starts to brown, 5 to 8 minutes. Add ½ cup water and the cream, scrape the pan, and bring to a bare simmer. Cover the pan, reduce the heat to low, and simmer the bacon cream for 20 minutes, scraping the bottom of the pot occasionally.

Use a slotted spoon or a strainer to remove all the bacon from the pan, and discard the bacon. Cool the cream until it is lukewarm. Then, using a stick blender, blend the cream for about 1 minute to help homogenize the cream and bacon fat. Reserve the bacon cream in the fridge.

Combine the sugar, corn syrup, and ¼ cup water in a medium saucepan, and stir until all of the sugar looks wet. Cover, put the pan over medium-high heat, and cook, stirring occasionally, until the sugar has completely melted, about 3 minutes.

Continue to cook, covered but this time without stirring, until the mixture has thickened slightly, about 3 minutes. Remove the lid and continue cooking, without stirring but paying close attention, until the mixture turns the color of dark maple syrup, about 5 minutes more.

Take the pan off the heat, and immediately pour in the bacon cream in a nice steady stream (whatever you do, do not dump it all in at once!), whisking as you pour. It'll bubble furiously.

Put the pan over medium-high heat again. Attach a candy thermometer to the side of the pan. Let the mixture simmer away, stirring it occasionally, until it registers 232°F on the thermometer, 5 to 8 minutes. Take the pan off the heat and add the butter and salt, stirring slowly but constantly until the butter has completely melted.

Let the caramel cool to room temperature before using, or transfer it to an airtight container and store it in the fridge for up to 2 weeks. Before using, gently reheat until drizzleable. Separation is totally normal; just make sure to stir it well before using it.

CHOCOLATE NOUGAT CRÈME

MAKES ABOUT 2½ CUPS

3 large egg whites (no specks of yolk allowed!)

½ teaspoon cream of tartar

⅔ cup light corn syrup

¼ cup granulated sugar

1½ teaspoons unflavored powdered gelatin

1 tablespoon unsweetened cocoa powder

If you've ever had a frozen Snickers bar, you know how sub-32°F temperatures turn nougat from soft and chewy to hurts-your-teeth hard. I kind of love that sensation, but what if we could make nougat that stayed supple in the freezer? The answer is this nougat crème: whipped egg whites sweetened and stiffened by syrup, then set with gelatin. It's basically homemade marshmallow without the waiting, dusting, and cutting.

In a stand mixer fitted with the whisk attachment, beat the egg whites on medium-high speed until they look foamy. Add the cream of tartar and continue to beat until the whites reach soft peak stage (lifting the whisk will create a little mountain of egg whites, but its pointy peak will immediately flop over), about 3 minutes. Reduce the mixer speed to the lowest setting and let that run while you make the sugar syrup.

Mix the corn syrup, sugar, and ¼ cup water in a medium saucepan and attach a candy thermometer to the pan. Cook over medium-high heat, stirring constantly, until the syrup goes from cloudy to clear. Stop stirring and continue heating on medium-high until the syrup reaches 238°F on the thermometer. Immediately remove the pan from the heat, raise the mixer speed to medium-low, and drizzle the hot sugar syrup into the egg whites in the mixer bowl in a thin, steady stream, aiming for a spot inside the bowl about ½ inch from the rim. (Reserve the pan you used for the syrup.) Once the syrup is well combined, increase the speed to medium-high and beat until the mixture looks glossy and has cooled until it's just warm to the touch, about 3 minutes.

While the sugar is whipping, bloom the gelatin by combining it with 1 tablespoon cold water in a small cup. Stir, and let the gelatin sit in the water until it completely hydrates and begins to soften, about 1 minute. Once it has bloomed, add the gelatin to the reserved (still warm) syrup pan and stir until the gelatin completely melts and becomes a clear syrup.

After the mixture gets its beautiful sheen, drizzle in the gelatin syrup and mix on medium-high speed for about 1 minute. (Pouring it through a strainer helps keep the stream consistent.) Use a fine-mesh strainer to sift in the cocoa powder, then mix until it is completely combined, about 1 minute. Transfer to an airtight container and use it immediately or store it for up to 1 week in the fridge. Before using, stir to loosen the crème.

DANDELION CHOCOLATE'S ROASTED CACAO BEAN GELATO

MAKES ABOUT
1½
PINTS

Each bar from Dandelion Chocolate, a small-batch chocolate maker in San Francisco, begins with carefully sourced beans, fermented and dried by farmers in places like Ambanja, Madagascar, and Punta Gorda, Belize. The result is chocolate that swaps uninspiring uniformity (hello, grocery-checkout-line chocolate!) for compelling complexity. Our homage to their process showcases whole cacao beans, incorporating the earthy, smoky hull of the bean, the nibs (the inside of the bean that's actually ground and sweetened to make chocolate), and the finished product. We churn it into gelato, which is denser and has less fat than ice cream and therefore packs more flavor per scoop, to ensure that all that complexity comes through. If you can score whole roasted cacao beans with the hull—bean-to-bar companies occasionally sell them—whack them with a rolling pin to make nib-size pieces. Otherwise, you can just use nibs and chocolate from a great maker and still get this cool interplay: the earthy astringency of the former and the sweet, roasty, fruity flavors of the latter. For super synergy (and extra credit), make sure both come from beans of the same origin.

1⅓ cups whole milk

⅔ cup heavy cream

½ cup cacao nibs

½ cup granulated sugar

5 large egg yolks

2 tablespoons finely chopped Dandelion Chocolate or another bright, complex chocolate

1 teaspoon kosher salt

⅛ teaspoon xanthan gum (Yes, I'm easy to find! See page 33.)

Combine the milk, cream, cacao nibs, and ¼ cup of the sugar in a small saucepan and bring to a simmer over medium-high heat, stirring frequently. Reduce the heat to maintain a lazy simmer and cook, stirring often, until the cocoa flavor has infused into the cream and the mixture is light brown, about 15 minutes. Remove from the heat. Strain the mixture through a fine-mesh sieve set over a heatproof container and discard the solids. Cover to keep it warm.

In a medium mixing bowl, combine the egg yolks and the remaining ¼ cup sugar and whisk vigorously until slightly frothy, about 2 minutes. (Here's a tip: Steady the bowl by wrapping a damp kitchen towel around the base.) Then slowly pour the warm milk mixture into the bowl while whisking constantly. Transfer the mixture to the saucepan and cook on medium-low heat, stirring constantly, until it thickens enough to coat the back of a spoon, about 2 minutes. Remove from the heat.

Stir the chocolate, salt, and xanthan gum into the mixture and continue to whisk until the chocolate is fully melted and the mixture is smooth. Let the mixture cool to room temperature, then chill it in the fridge overnight if you are using a frozen-bowl type of machine. It will keep, refrigerated, for up to 3 days.

(recipe continues)

Stir the base and pour the mixture into an ice cream maker and turn on the machine. Churn just until the mixture has the texture of a pourable frozen smoothie (see pages 23 to 24 for timing ranges, depending on the machine).

Quickly transfer the gelato, scraping every last delicious drop from the machine, into freezer-friendly containers. Cover with parchment paper, pressing it to the surface of the gelato so it adheres, then cover with a lid. It's okay if the parchment hangs over the rim. Store it in the coldest part of your freezer (farthest from the door) until firm, at least 6 hours. It will keep for up to 3 months.

CINNAMON SNICKERDOODLE

MAKES ABOUT

2½

PINTS

An unassuming triumph like the snickerdoodle cookie deserves an ice cream that celebrates its simplicity. We churn our famously high-fat ice cream with cinnamon, plus a little salt and fruity ancho chile powder to help tame all that sweetness.

What makes our version so yummy is the top-notch cinnamon we get from Red Ape—an outfit in Eugene, Oregon, that grinds spices in small batches, though as long as you ditch the dusty jar on your shelf for something fresh, you'll get the idea—and the crumbles of buttery, cinnamony cookies that we design specifically to be frozen in ice cream without losing their chewy texture.

WHAT WE LEARN: *Mixing delicious things into ice cream isn't always as simple as it sounds. Take the cookies in this flavor. We need to anticipate how they'll be* after *freezing. Regular cookies would end up unpleasantly hard, so we make ours with extra cream of tartar and baking soda, which helps the cookies puff up more; the extra-light texture makes it so the cookies soak up just the right amount of cream. When they're frozen, they have the same tender, moist texture they did when you pulled them from the oven. Keep that in mind when you're baking for your own batch of cookie ice cream!*

3 cups Ice Cream Base (page 34), very cold

4 teaspoons ground cinnamon

Pinch kosher salt

Pinch ancho chile powder

1 cup crumbled Snickerdoodle Cookies (recipe follows)

In a bowl, combine the ice cream base, cinnamon, salt, and ancho chile powder and whisk until the spices are well combined with the base. Let the mixture sit for 10 to 15 minutes in the refrigerator to let the spices fully saturate.

Whisk the mixture briefly again, then pour it into an ice cream maker and turn on the machine. Churn just until it has the texture of soft-serve (see pages 23 to 24 for timing ranges, depending on the machine).

Quickly transfer the ice cream, scraping every last delicious drop from the machine, into freezer-friendly containers: Spoon in a layer of ice cream, sprinkle on some snickerdoodle crumbles, and use a spoon to press them in gently. Repeat. Cover with parchment paper, pressing it to the surface of the ice cream so it adheres, then cover with a lid. It's okay if the parchment hangs over the rim. Store it in the coldest part of your freezer (farthest from the door) until firm, at least 6 hours. It will keep for up to 3 months.

SNICKERDOODLE COOKIES

MAKES ABOUT 7 CUPS OF COOKIE CRUMBLES

8 tablespoons
  (1 stick) unsalted
  butter, at room
  temperature

1 cup plus
  3 tablespoons
  granulated sugar

1 large egg, at room
  temperature

1½ cups all-purpose
  flour

2 teaspoons cream
  of tartar

1 teaspoon baking
  soda

1 teaspoon kosher
  salt

1½ teaspoons ground
  cinnamon

Combine the butter and the 1 cup sugar in a stand mixer fitted with the paddle attachment, and mix on high speed, scraping down the sides as necessary, until it becomes slightly airy and turns a shade lighter, about 3 minutes. Add the egg and mix until completely combined.

In a large bowl, whisk the flour, cream of tartar, baking soda, and salt to combine and make sure there aren't any lumps. Add the flour mixture to the stand mixer and mix on medium-low speed until the flour is incorporated and you have a crumbly dough. Press the dough together to form a disk, wrap it in plastic wrap, and refrigerate it until chilled, at least 2 hours or ideally overnight.

Heat the oven to 375°F. Line a sheet pan with parchment and spray it with nonstick spray.

Mix the remaining 3 tablespoons sugar and the cinnamon in a wide bowl until thoroughly combined. Roll the cold cookie dough into golf-ball-size pieces. One by one, add them to the sugar mixture, toss to coat them, and transfer them to the prepared sheet pan, leaving about an inch of space between them. Bake, rotating the sheet pan halfway through, until the cookies are golden around the edges and the tops crack, about 20 minutes. Use a spatula to transfer them to a cooling rack and let them cool completely.

Crumble the cookies into ¼- to ½-inch pieces. The cookies will keep in an airtight container at room temperature for 1 week.

SEA SALT WITH CARAMEL RIBBONS

MAKES ABOUT
2
PINTS

Salted caramel has become the kale salad of ice cream flavors—every scoop shop has its version. I'm certainly not immune to the sweet-salty pleasures (I like kale salad, too!), but I decided to reimagine the classic. Instead of merging salted caramel with the ice cream, I spike top-quality dairy with just enough salt to bring out its nuances and make it the star of the show. Then I drizzle in luscious ribbons of caramel.

Thanks to Mark Bitterman of The Meadow—my salt Yoda (see page 8) and the guy who, literally, wrote the book on the subject—I learned that the type of salt you use has a major impact on the finished product. I use his own *fleur de sel*, which is made in Guatemala from the same salt plains famed for supplying the Mayan empire at the height of its power. I suggest you nerd out like I did, investing in a variety of sea salts from different places and sampling each one mixed with cream.

1¼ teaspoons fleur de sel

3 cups Ice Cream Base (page 34), very cold

½ cup Perfect Ice Cream Caramel (recipe follows)

Combine ¼ cup water and the fleur de sel in a small saucepan, set it over medium heat, and cook, stirring, just until the salt has completely dissolved, less than 1 minute. Let it cool to room temperature.

Put the ice cream base and the salt mixture into a bowl and whisk to combine. Pour the mixture into an ice cream maker and turn on the machine. Churn just until the mixture has the texture of soft-serve (see pages 23 to 24 for timing ranges, depending on the machine).

Put the caramel in a warm place or warm it in a small saucepan over very low heat just until it's drizzleable, but not so warm that it'll melt the ice cream.

Quickly alternate spooning layers of the ice cream and drizzling on a generous spiral of caramel in freezer-friendly containers.

Cover with parchment paper, pressing it to the surface of the ice cream so it adheres, then cover with a lid. It's okay if the parchment hangs over the rim. Store it in the coldest part of your freezer (farthest from the door) until firm, at least 6 hours. It will keep for up to 3 months.

PERFECT ICE CREAM CARAMEL

MAKES ABOUT 1¾ CUPS

- 1½ cups granulated sugar
- ¼ cup light corn syrup
- 1¼ cups heavy cream
- 2 tablespoons unsalted butter, cut into several pieces
- ½ teaspoon kosher salt

Making delicious caramel sauce is easy. But making caramel that will remain chewy, sticky, and liquidy when suspended in ice cream? Well, it turns out that's easy, too! It just takes a little extra simmering. I owe this revelation to chocolatier, candy maker, and all-around cool guy David Briggs of Portland's Xocolatl de David. When my caramel began mysteriously sinking to the bottom of the ice cream I made, it was David who saved the day.

The first step is to create flavor by cooking the sugar, melting and busting apart the sweet but flavor-free sucrose molecules into bits that bounce around and create tinier, tastier compounds. The result is much less sweet and much more yummy from toasty, acidic, and bitter flavors. Before, I would add cream and call it a day. But now I know to continue cooking, to evaporate some of the water in the cream, to achieve the right density, so the caramel stays put as it freezes and retains its magical texture.

CARAMEL (NOT QUITE) FOREVER!

Here's a neat trick to extend the caramel's shelf life from 2 weeks to 2 months: While it's still super hot, pour the caramel into one or several sanitized Ball jars and screw on the lids. Turn the jars upside down and let the caramel cool. As it does, it'll create an airtight seal, no pot of boiling water necessary!

Combine the sugar, corn syrup, and ¼ cup water in a medium saucepan, and stir until all of the sugar looks wet. Cover, set the pan over medium-high heat, and cook, stirring occasionally, until the sugar has completely melted, about 3 minutes.

Continue to cook, covered but this time without stirring, until the mixture has thickened slightly, about 3 minutes. Remove the lid and continue cooking, without stirring but paying close attention, until the mixture turns the color of dark maple syrup, about 5 minutes more.

Take the pan off the heat and immediately and *gradually* pour in the cream, going slowly at first and then speeding up to a nice steady stream, whisking as you pour.

Put the pan over medium-high heat again. Attach a candy thermometer to the side of the pan. Let the mixture simmer away, stirring it occasionally, until it registers 230°F on the thermometer, about 3 minutes. Take the pan off the heat and add the butter and salt, stirring slowly but constantly until the butter has completely melted.

Let the caramel cool to room temperature, then use it right away or transfer it to an airtight container and refrigerate it for up to 2 weeks. Separation is totally normal; just make sure to stir the caramel well before using it.

ALMOND BRITTLE
WITH SALTED GANACHE

MAKES ABOUT
2½
PINTS

My grandma's famous almond brittle joins forces with slightly salty, chocolatey blobs of ganache to make a flavor that's oh-my-ganache good. Ganache is super easy to make at home and basically the same as the inside of a chocolate truffle: a blend of cream and chocolate. It stays soft and creamy when frozen, so you don't get any weird waxy chocolate bits. Just the right amount of salt brings all the toffee-y, chocolatey, toasted almond flavors together. There'd be riots in Portland if we took it off the menu. So we just keep making more.

3 cups Ice Cream
Base (page 34),
very cold

¼ teaspoon vanilla
extract

¾ cup Grandma
Malek's Almond
Brittle pieces
(recipe follows)

¾ cup Salted
Ganache (recipe
follows), cut into
small cubes

Put the ice cream base and the vanilla into a bowl and whisk to combine. Pour the mixture into an ice cream maker. Turn on the machine. Churn just until the mixture has the texture of soft-serve (see pages 23 to 24 for timing ranges, depending on the machine).

Quickly transfer the ice cream to freezer-friendly containers: Spoon in a layer of ice cream, sprinkle on the almond brittle and salted ganache, and use a spoon to press them in gently. Repeat.

Cover with parchment paper, pressing it to the surface of the ice cream so it adheres, then cover with a lid. It's okay if the parchment hangs over the rim. Store it in the coldest part of your freezer (farthest from the door) until firm, at least 6 hours. It will keep for up to 2 months.

GRANDMA MALEK'S ALMOND BRITTLE

MAKES ABOUT 3 CUPS OF BRITTLE PIECES

1 cup granulated
sugar

¹/₃ cup light corn
syrup

8 tablespoons
(1 stick) unsalted
butter, cut into
approximately
1-inch pieces

¹/₂ teaspoon kosher
salt

1¹/₄ cups sliced
almonds

1 teaspoon baking
soda

¹/₂ teaspoon vanilla
extract

In the early days of Salt & Straw, I called and asked my grandma if she'd give me the recipe for her almond brittle. Her response: "Why?" Why, Grandma Malek? Because your chewy-crunchy almonds encased in buttery candy are glorious, one of the yummiest memories of my entire childhood. It helped launch one of our most popular flavors. Now we make her brittle in Willy Wonka Factory–size batches and most of Portland knows her by name. She still asks me if we have to double her original recipe to make enough. Grandma, you have no idea.

Line a sheet pan with parchment paper or a silicone baking mat.

Combine the sugar, corn syrup, and ¼ cup water in a medium saucepan and stir until all of the sugar looks wet. Set the pan over medium heat and cook, stirring occasionally, until the syrup comes to a simmer, about 3 minutes.

Continue to cook, this time covered and without stirring, until the mixture has thickened slightly, about 3 more minutes. Add the butter and salt, and stir well. Attach a candy thermometer to the side of the pan and continue to cook, gently and constantly stirring, until the mixture registers 290°F on the thermometer, 8 to 10 minutes.

Remove the pan from the heat, and quickly but thoroughly stir in the almonds, baking soda, and vanilla (watch it all bubble!), doing your best to distribute the nuts throughout the sticky mixture. Immediately (like, super quick!) pour the mixture onto the lined sheet pan and use a butter knife or a metal spatula to spread it out to a relatively even layer that's just under ¼ inch thick.

Let the brittle sit uncovered until it has cooled to room temperature, about 1 hour. Then use your hands to break it into irregular bite-size (about ¼- to ½-inch) pieces. Store them in an airtight container in the freezer until you're ready to use them as a mix-in (or to simply eat them) for up to 3 months. There's no need to defrost the pieces before using them in the ice cream.

SALTED GANACHE

MAKES ABOUT 1 CUP

⅔ cup heavy cream

1 tablespoon granulated sugar

1 cup chopped chocolate (chip-size), preferably 80% or darker

1 teaspoon kosher salt

As far as ice cream mix-ins go, chocolate chips have nothing on ganache. And great news: Ganache is so much easier to make than its French name might suggest. You just melt chocolate in cream, then whisk or blend to turn two slightly reluctant fats into fast friends. The rich, silky product tastes like the chocolate icing of your dreams and stays smooth and creamy even after freezing. I salt it generously because it tastes so good that way.

Combine the cream and sugar in a medium saucepan, stir well, and bring the mixture to a bare simmer over medium heat, stirring occasionally. Remove the pan from the heat, add the chocolate and salt, and let it sit, stirring and scraping the pan occasionally, until the chocolate begins to melt, about 2 minutes.

Use a sturdy whisk to vigorously stir until the chocolate has completely melted and the mixture becomes smooth and satiny, about 1 minute. Congratulations, you just made ganache!

Transfer the ganache to an airtight container and store it in the freezer for at least 2 hours or up to 1 month. There's no need to defrost it before using.

STRAWBERRY HONEY BALSAMIC WITH BLACK PEPPER

MAKES ABOUT

2

PINTS

A scoop of strawberry ice cream doesn't taste much like strawberry, does it? Don't get me wrong, the classic flavor has its place, but once you've added enough fat to make ice cream properly creamy, you've obscured the bright qualities that makes the berry so loveable. In my world, evading the Strawberry Problem is a fun challenge, one that has spurred all sorts of solutions during the life of Salt & Straw. Perhaps our favorite is inspired by the Italian way of enjoying the fruit. By adding balsamic to reclaim its acidity and black pepper to play up its fruitiness, we recreate the texture and richness of the classic, just with more strawberry oomph.

WHAT WE LEARN: *Mixing in jams after churning is a great way to incorporate fruity flavors into ice cream. Jams are cool because they're cooked to make a concentrated version of the fruit and because their high sugar content means they never freeze, so each swirl delivers its flavor immediately—before the rich ice cream registers.*

¾ cup Strawberry Puree (recipe follows), very cold

¼ cup honey balsamic vinegar, like Honey Ridge Farms or O Olive Oil

⅛ teaspoon freshly (and very finely) ground black pepper

3 cups Ice Cream Base (page 34), very cold

¾ cup your favorite strawberry jam

In a bowl, combine the strawberry puree, vinegar, and black pepper with the ice cream base. Whisk as needed to get everything completely incorporated into the base. Pour the mixture into an ice cream maker and turn on the machine. Churn just until it has the texture of soft-serve (see pages 23 to 24 for timing ranges, depending on the machine).

Stir the jam with a fork to loosen it. Quickly alternate spooning layers of the mixture and dollops of the jam in freezer-friendly containers.

Cover with parchment paper, pressing it to the surface of the ice cream so it adheres, then cover with a lid. It's okay if the parchment hangs over the rim. Store it in the coldest part of your freezer (farthest from the door) until firm, at least 6 hours. It will keep for up to 3 months.

STRAWBERRY PUREE

MAKES ABOUT ¾ CUP

10 ounces (about 1 pint) ripe strawberries, hulled and halved

¼ cup honey

Heat the oven to 300°F. Line a sheet pan with parchment paper.

Spread the strawberries out evenly on the lined sheet pan and drizzle them with the honey. Bake for 15 minutes. Stir the berries and continue baking until they just barely begin to caramelize and get a little bit of roasted color to them, about 20 minutes more. Remove the sheet pan from the oven and let them sit until they're cool enough to handle. Transfer the berries to a blender along with the yummy sticky stuff on the parchment paper and puree to make a smooth sauce. Chill in the fridge until cold.

Store the puree in the fridge for up to 2 weeks or in the freezer for up to 3 months.

PEAR & BLUE CHEESE

MAKES ABOUT
2½
PINTS

We celebrate the heck out of two Oregon products in this scoop: Cave-aged Crater Lake blue from Rogue Creamery gets the cheese-plate treatment when it's paired with local pears. And boy does our state grow a lot of them, including some of the best dang Bartletts in the world. We take this winning combination from the savory world and bring it into sweet frozen territory—and it fits right in. Use the boldest blue you can find so it'll stand strong against the sweetness and keep each bite balanced.

WHAT WE LEARN: *Like so many fruits, pears have a delicate flavor that can get muffled by the butterfat you need for a proper ice cream. Tempting as it is to solve the problem by packing the mixture with ever more pear, this strategy risks adding too much sugar and water to the base, either of which could mess with the texture of the ice cream. My answer? Candying pears to mix in after churning, which gives each bite a hit of the fruit that's bold enough to punch through all that cream. The technique also works well with apples, peaches, and apricots.*

¼ cup pea-size pieces of Rogue Creamery Crater Lake blue cheese or the creamy, sweet, super blue cheese of your choice

3 cups Ice Cream Base (page 34), very cold

¾ cup Pear Puree (recipe follows), very cold

¾ cup Candied Pears (recipe follows)

Put the blue cheese on a plate lined with parchment paper, cover with plastic wrap, put the plate in the freezer, until the cheese pieces are frozen solid (so they won't completely blend into the ice cream), at least 45 minutes. If a few pieces freeze together, that's fine; just gently break them apart.

Put the ice cream base and the pear puree into a bowl and whisk to combine. Pour the mixture into an ice cream maker and turn on the machine. Churn just until the mixture has the texture of soft-serve (see pages 23 to 24 for timing ranges, depending on the machine).

Quickly transfer the ice cream to freezer-friendly containers: Spoon in a layer of ice cream, sprinkle on some candied pears and frozen blue cheese, and use a spoon to press them in gently. Repeat. Cover with parchment paper, pressing it to the surface of the ice cream so it adheres, then cover with a lid. It's okay if the parchment hangs over the rim. Store it in the coldest part of your freezer (farthest from the door) until firm, at least 6 hours. It will keep for up to 3 months.

PEAR PUREE

MAKES ABOUT ¾ CUP

1 cup peeled and
diced slightly
underripe pear,
preferably
Bartlett

¼ cup granulated
sugar

1 small cinnamon
stick

Pinch kosher salt

Pinch ground nutmeg

In a small saucepan, combine the diced pear, sugar, ½ cup water, the cinnamon stick, salt, and nutmeg. Set it over medium heat, and bring to a simmer. Reduce the heat to low and cook, stirring occasionally, until the pear cubes are falling apart and incredibly tender, about 45 minutes. Remove the cinnamon stick and let the mixture cool to room temperature.

Transfer to a blender and puree the mixture until it's perfectly smooth. Chill it thoroughly in the fridge before using, or store it, covered, in the fridge for up to 1 week or in the freezer for up to 3 months.

CANDIED PEARS

MAKES ABOUT ¾ CUP

3 cups granulated
sugar

1 cup peeled and
diced (¼- to
½-inch) slightly
underripe pear,
preferably
Bartletts

In a small saucepan, heat 1 cup of the sugar and 1 cup water over medium-high heat until the sugar has completely dissolved, creating a clear simple syrup. Reduce the heat to low so the syrup just steams and add the diced pear. Let the mixture steep, without simmering, for 20 minutes. Remove the pan from the heat, cover with a lid, and let it sit at room temperature for 1 hour.

Strain the pears from their syrup, set the pears aside, and discard the syrup (or use it for cocktails). Put the remaining 2 cups sugar and 1 cup water in the same saucepan and heat over medium-high heat until the sugar has completely dissolved. Reduce the heat to low and add the diced pears. Let the mixture steep on low heat without simmering for 20 minutes, until the pears are saturated with sugar and slightly translucent but still intact. Remove the pan from the heat, cover it with a lid, and let sit at room temperature for about 1 hour.

Transfer the pears in their syrup to an airtight container and refrigerate until cold or for up to 2 weeks. Strain them before using. The pears can also be stored in the freezer for up to 6 months; thaw and strain before using.

DOUBLE-FOLD VANILLA

MAKES ABOUT
1½
PINTS

When you're known for serving flavors like Pear & Blue Cheese (page 81) and Salted Caramel Thanksgiving Turkey (page 209), introducing a familiar flavor to your lineup causes quite a stir. So when we finally decided to make vanilla ice cream, we knew it had to impress. We sourced top-notch double-strength extract ("double fold" in industry lingo) from our friends at Singing Dog Vanilla in Eugene, Oregon. We love that they not only work with growers in Papua New Guinea and Indonesia to produce the exceptional organic vanilla but also give these farmers a fair price and a share of the profits. Plus, offering vanilla at our shops gives us a chance to show off the ice cream we're so proud of, the flavor being familiar enough for customers to be able to focus on the texture of a Salt & Straw scoop. Since our base maxes out ice cream's butterfat content, you get to enjoy the complex, expensive vanilla flavor on your palate for a luxuriously long time.

WHAT WE LEARN: *Vanilla is an ingredient that doesn't get the love it deserves. It's one of the most complex natural flavors on earth, with, oh, around 250 chemical compounds contributing to its pleasures. Cheap imitation vanilla extracts abound, and in case you're tempted to think the cheaper the better, I have two words of caution: beaver butts. (Look it up.) A taste of the good stuff, whether from the seeds themselves or in a pure vanilla (not vanillin) extract, is a revelation. You'll never use the word "vanilla" as a synonym for "plain" ever again.*

3 cups Ice Cream Base (page 34), very cold

2 teaspoons double-fold vanilla extract, preferably from Singing Dog or homemade (recipe follows)

Put the ice cream base and the vanilla into a bowl and whisk to combine. Pour the mixture into an ice cream maker and turn on the machine. Churn just until the mixture has the texture of soft-serve (see pages 23 to 24 for timing ranges, depending on the machine).

Quickly transfer the ice cream, scraping every last delicious drop from the machine, into freezer-friendly containers. Cover with parchment paper, pressing it to the surface of the ice cream so it adheres, then cover with a lid. It's okay if the parchment hangs over the rim. Store it in the coldest part of your freezer (farthest from the door) until firm, at least 6 hours. It will keep for up to 3 months.

HOMEMADE VANILLA EXTRACT

MAKES ABOUT 1 CUP

Ten 6- to 7-inch-
long vanilla beans

1 cup 80-proof vodka
(get good stuff
without too much
of its own flavor,
like Grey Goose)

Note that this extract needs to be prepped 1 month before using.

Slice the beans in half lengthwise. Put them in a 12- to 16-ounce glass jar and add the vodka. Push the beans down so they are fully submerged.

Store the glass jar in a cool, dark place for 30 days, shaking it gently every few days. After 30 days, strain the liquid, pressing on the beans to extract as much liquid as you can. Discard the beans. Store the extract in an airtight glass container and use within 1 year.

ROASTED STRAWBERRY & TOASTED WHITE CHOCOLATE

MAKES ABOUT

3

PINTS

Time-travel back to the late aughts, when Salt & Straw was just a glimmer in our eyes and when toasted white chocolate was on every fancy restaurant's pastry menu. Return to those heady days when you squeezed into your first pair of skinny jeans and indulged in that first taste of sweet, mellow white chocolate that had been caramelized to dulce-de-leche-esque complexity. Add swirls of roasted-strawberry jam and this flavor is as irresistible as a Kanye–Taylor Swift dustup.

1 cup white chocolate chips or chopped white chocolate (Hershey's is our favorite!)

1/2 cup heavy cream

1 tablespoon granulated sugar

1 large egg yolk

1 teaspoon kosher salt

1 teaspoon vanilla extract, preferably Mexican

3 cups Ice Cream Base (page 34), very cold

3/4 cup Roasted Strawberry Jam (recipe follows)

Heat the oven to 350°F.

Line a sheet pan with parchment paper and spread the white chocolate chips out on it in an even layer. Bake for 5 to 8 minutes, stirring occasionally to ensure that the chocolate caramelizes evenly. Once it's evenly browned to a dark gold, take it out of the oven.

Put the cream in a small saucepan and cook over medium-high heat until it's hot to the touch, about 3 minutes. In a bowl, whisk together the sugar and egg yolk. Once the cream is ready, remove it from the heat and add the white chocolate, salt, and vanilla. Blend with a stick blender and add the sugar-yolk mixture. Let cool to room temperature.

Put the ice cream base and the toasted white chocolate mixture in a bowl and whisk until well combined. Chill in the fridge until cold. (It will keep for up to 4 days.)

Pour the mixture into an ice cream maker and turn on the machine. Churn just until the mixture has the texture of soft-serve (see pages 23 to 24 for timing ranges, depending on the machine).

Stir the jam with a fork to loosen it. Quickly alternate spooning layers of the mixture and a dollop of the jam in freezer-friendly containers.

Cover with parchment paper, pressing it to the surface of the ice cream so it adheres, then cover with a lid. It's okay if the parchment hangs over the rim. Store it in the coldest part of your freezer (farthest from the door) until firm, at least 6 hours. It will keep for up to 3 months.

ROASTED STRAWBERRY JAM

MAKES ABOUT ¾ CUP

2 cups ripe
  strawberries,
  hulled and cut
  into ⅛- to
  ¼-inch slices

6 tablespoons
  granulated sugar

2 teaspoons freshly
  squeezed lemon
  juice

Put the strawberries on a sheet pan, sprinkle them with the sugar and the lemon juice, and toss everything together to ensure that the berries are completely covered in sugar. Spread them out in an even layer and let them sit at room temperature for about 15 minutes so the berries macerate a bit.

Meanwhile, heat the oven to 350°F.

Stir the berries, put the sheet pan in the oven, and bake, stirring them every 5 minutes or so, until they are very soft and the juices are syrupy, about 20 minutes. Make sure the strawberries don't caramelize at all.

Remove the sheet pan from the oven, transfer the berries and their juices to a heatproof bowl, and use the back of a spoon to lightly mash the strawberries to make a chunky jam. Cool to room temperature. Store in the fridge for up to 1 week or in the freezer for up to 3 months.

SALTED CARAMEL BARS & COCONUT CREAM

MAKES ABOUT

3

PINTS

Lisa Clark opened Petunia's Pies & Pastries as a tribute to her mother's baking and as salvation for those who, like Lisa herself, love yummy things but whose bodies don't always agree with dairy or gluten. Her salted caramel bars—made with banana, almond flour, and dairy-free caramel—showed us that vegans and people with gluten sensitivity can totally eat delicious things. In collaboration with Lisa and her team, we devised an ice cream–friendly version of her famous bars, which we stir into a coconut base along with swirls of chocolate ganache (engineered with almond milk!) and caramel (concocted with coconut cream!). When you serve it to the one remaining person you know who thinks vegan food can't be good, don't tell him what's in it until he's finished his third bowl.

4 cups Coconut Ice Cream Base (page 39), very cold

1 teaspoon vanilla extract

½ teaspoon kosher salt

¾ cup Almond Milk Ganache (recipe follows)

½ cup Coconut Cream Caramel (recipe follows)

¾ cup chopped Salted Caramel Bars (recipe follows)

Put the coconut ice cream base, vanilla, and salt into a bowl and whisk to combine. Pour the mixture into an ice cream maker and turn on the machine. Churn just until the mixture has the texture of soft-serve (see pages 23 to 24 for timing ranges, depending on the machine).

Quickly transfer the ice cream into freezer-friendly containers: Spoon in layers of ice cream, dollops of ganache, swirls of coconut cream caramel, and sprinkles of chopped caramel bars.

Cover with parchment paper, pressing it to the surface of the ice cream so it adheres, then cover with a lid. It's okay if the parchment hangs over the rim. Store it in the coldest part of your freezer (farthest from the door) until firm, at least 6 hours. It will keep for up to 3 months.

ALMOND MILK GANACHE

MAKES ABOUT 1 CUP

½ cup unflavored, unsweetened almond milk

2 tablespoons granulated sugar

1 cup semisweet or bittersweet chocolate chips

½ teaspoon kosher salt

Combine the almond milk and sugar in a medium saucepan, stir well, and bring to a lazy simmer over medium-high heat, stirring occasionally. Remove from the heat as soon as the mixture bubbles, add the chocolate and salt, and let it sit, stirring occasionally until the chocolate begins to melt, about 2 minutes.

Use a sturdy whisk to vigorously blend the mixture until the chocolate has completely melted and the mixture is smooth and satiny, about 1 minute.

Transfer the ganache to an airtight container and store it in the freezer for at least 2 hours or up to 1 month. There's no need to defrost it before using.

COCONUT CREAM CARAMEL

MAKES ABOUT 1¾ CUPS

1½ cups granulated sugar

¼ cup light corn syrup

¾ cup unsweetened coconut cream (preferably Aroy-D and boxed, not canned)

½ teaspoon kosher salt

Combine the sugar, corn syrup, and ¼ cup water in a medium saucepan, and stir until all of the sugar looks wet. Cover the pan, set it over medium-high heat, and cook, stirring occasionally, until the sugar has completely melted, about 3 minutes.

Continue to cook, covered but this time without stirring, until the mixture has thickened slightly, about 3 minutes. Remove the lid and continue cooking, without stirring but paying close attention, until the mixture turns the color of dark maple syrup, about 5 minutes more.

Take the pan off the heat and immediately and *gradually* pour in the coconut cream, going slowly at first and then speeding up to a nice steady stream, whisking as you pour. It'll bubble furiously, so stand back!

Put the pan over medium-high heat again. Attach a candy thermometer to the side of the pan. Let the mixture simmer away, stirring it occasionally, until it registers 235°F on the thermometer, about 3 minutes. Take the pan off the heat and add the salt, stirring slowly for 30 seconds to make sure the salt mixes in completely.

Let the caramel cool to room temperature, then transfer it to an airtight container. Store it at room temperature for up to 2 weeks. Separation is totally normal—just make sure to stir it well before using it.

SALTED CARAMEL BARS

MAKES ABOUT 4 CUPS OF CHOPPED BARS

1 tablespoon egg replacer (preferably Bob's Red Mill)

½ cup Earth Balance buttery spread, melted

1 cup (lightly packed) light brown sugar

½ cup mashed very ripe bananas

2 teaspoons vanilla extract

1¼ cups 1-to-1 gluten-free flour (preferably Bob's Red Mill)

½ teaspoon baking soda

½ teaspoon kosher salt

1 cup slivered chocolate, from a chocolate bar (not chips)

½ cup Coconut Cream Caramel (opposite)

2 teaspoons fleur de sel or another flaky salt

Heat the oven to 350°F. Lightly spray an 8 × 8-inch baking pan with nonstick cooking spray.

In a small cup, mix the egg replacer with 2 tablespoons water and set it aside to allow it to "activate."

In a stand mixer fitted with the paddle attachment, beat the melted Earth Balance, brown sugar, and bananas on medium speed until the mixture looks lighter in color, about 3 minutes. Reduce the speed to low, add the vanilla and egg replacer, then increase the speed to medium-high and mix until completely combined.

In a separate mixing bowl, lightly whisk together the flour, baking soda, and salt, breaking up any clumps. Turn off the stand mixer, add the flour mixture to the egg mixture, then mix on medium speed until the ingredients are just combined. Use a large spoon to fold the chocolate slivers into the batter.

Pour about half of the batter into the prepared baking pan and spread it in an even layer. Pour the caramel over the top, sprinkle with the fleur de sel, and use a large spoon to gently dollop the remaining batter on top. Bake until a butter knife inserted into the center comes out clean, about 30 minutes. Let the bars cool completely in the pan, then cut them into ½-inch pieces. Freeze on a tray or plate until solid, then use right away or transfer to freezer bags and store for up to 2 months.

Beer Name: Dylan's Lavender Beer		Target/Time	Actual
Grist		130 lbs	✓
GWM Two-Row		20 lbs	✓
Bob's Flaked Wheat		10 lbs	✓
Fawcett Torrified Wheat		10 lbs	
Simpsons Maris Otter			
			11:42
Mash/Lauter		30 min	11:43
			12:37
Mash Start			
Vorlauf Start		26 inches	1.044
Lauter Start		1.044	
Lauter End			
Kettle Full Depth			
Pre Boil Gravity			2.39
			2:45
Boil and Castout		3 squirts	2:59
FermCap S		60 min	3.55
Boil Start Time and Length			
Boil End Time			
Post Boil Volume		Y N	
Castout Start Time			
Castout End Time			
Aeration This Batch			
		0001/7	3:40
		8.4#	
Yeast		66 deg F	
Yeast Strain/Gen #			44 ppm Ca+
Pitch Weight			
Temperature into FV			
Specs			
1.046/1.010 > 4.7% ABV 20 IBU			

CHAPTER 3

THE
BREWER'S
SERIES

One day I decided to make beer ice cream. Simple, right? That's what I thought. But you can't just combine beer and cream. Okay, you can, but it typically doesn't work out very well. Beer is delicious, but its flavor just isn't concentrated enough to stand up to ice cream's high fat content. And if you try to cook off some of the water in order to intensify the flavor, you distort the character of the very beer you were trying to feature in the first place. Celebrating different beers in ice cream—that is, figuring out how to deconstruct each one and put it back together in sweet, creamy form so the brewer's original water-based creation is accurately reflected in each scoop—became one of my favorite ice cream–making puzzles.

In this chapter, you'll find my tastiest solutions. Don't be put off by all the hops, yeasts, and malt extracts—they're easy to find with a few clicks online or, even better, a trip to any of the growing number of shops devoted to home brewing.

There you'll find not just the ingredients but also people who will be pumped to help guide you to great substitutions if they don't stock a particular variety of hop. They'll be even more pumped once you tell them you're making beer ice cream.

INDIA PALE ALE

MAKES ABOUT

2½

PINTS

When I had the chance to shadow Ben Edmunds at Breakside Brewery, I did what I do best: asked a thousand questions. And he did what he does best: demonstrated his mastery of the subject of beer. I was particularly interested in IPAs, or India Pale Ales, so named because they were created some three centuries ago to survive the trip from England to colonizers in India. As a way of preventing spoilage, brewers added hops, a family of flowers that also imparts distinct flavors. Hops are used in many beers now, but their bitterness and aromatic qualities have come to define this particular style. Ben patiently took me through the varieties and taught me how to steep them to activate their best qualities. With his guidance, a scoop of this ice cream manages to capture the citrusy, tropical-fruit aromas of Citra, Chinook, and Falconer's Flight hops that are so pleasant in a pint glass.

WHAT WE LEARN: *Thanks to Ben, I learned that I could apply the nifty brewmaster's trick called dry hopping—basically, steeping hops in beer before bottling—to ice cream. If you let hops steep in water or cream, you won't get much flavor—a good extraction requires heat, which dulls their brightness and aromatic character. But when you steep hops in alcohol, whether it's the beer in traditional dry hopping or the vodka we use here, you can harness their fragrance. It's a neat trick that works any time you're trying to capture a fragrant ingredient in a scoop, be it vanilla or coffee. And leftover hop-infused vodka makes a great cocktail mixer, especially when combined with honey and citrus.*

¼ cup 100-proof unflavored alcohol, such as high-proof vodka

1 teaspoon Citra hop pellets

3 tablespoons golden light liquid malt extract

¼ cup caramel 40L malt, milled by a home brew shop

¼ cup caramel 20L malt, milled by a home brew shop

1 teaspoon Columbus hop pellets

At least one day in advance, combine the vodka and the Citra hops in a small glass jar, and cover it with an airtight lid. Steep for at least 24 and up to 36 hours.

Pour the vodka mixture through a fine-mesh strainer into a small bowl, pressing the solids lightly to extract as much liquid as possible. Reserve 1 tablespoon of the liquid for this recipe. The rest will keep in the fridge for up to 3 days.

In a small pot, bring 2 cups water to a rolling boil. Reduce the heat as low as it can go, then stir in the liquid malt extract, caramel 40L malt, caramel 20L malt, and Columbus hops. Cover and cook at a bare simmer, stirring occasionally, for 30 minutes. Then stir in the Falconer's Flight hops and cook for 15 minutes more. Finally add the Chinook hops and cook for 10 minutes. Remove the pot from the heat and pour the mixture through a fine-mesh strainer into a small heatproof bowl, pressing the solids lightly to extract as much liquid as possible.

(recipe continues)

1 teaspoon
  Falconer's Flight
  hop pellets

1 teaspoon Chinook
  hop pellets

3 cups Ice Cream
  Base (page 34),
  very cold

$1/2$ cup Breakside IPA
  or your favorite
  balanced, fruity-
  hopped IPA, cold

Fill another small mixing bowl with ice, then fill it halfway with water. Set the bowl containing the infused liquid into the ice water and stir to quickly cool the liquid. When it's cold, stir in the reserved 1 tablespoon infused vodka and use the syrup within 1 week.

Put the ice cream base, the cold beer, and ¾ cup of the cold IPA syrup into a bowl and whisk to combine. Pour the mixture into an ice cream maker and turn on the machine. Churn just until the mixture has the texture of soft-serve (see pages 23 to 24 for timing ranges, depending on the machine).

Transfer the ice cream, scraping every last delicious drop from the machine, into freezer-friendly containers. Cover with parchment paper, pressing it to the surface of the ice cream so it adheres, then cover with a lid. It's okay if the parchment hangs over the rim. Store it in the coldest part of your freezer (farthest from the door) until firm, at least 6 hours. It will keep for up to 3 months.

SMOKED HEFEWEIZEN

MAKES ABOUT

2½

PINTS

Our spin on Widmer Brothers' world-famous wheat ale employs their flavor-extraction techniques, so the sweet, malty flavors that I love about the beer are what hit you at first lick. We use smoked malts to balance the sugar and add a subtle, lingering, drinking-by-the-campfire quality that'll keep you hooked.

¼ cup wheat liquid malt extract

2 tablespoons caramel 40L malt, milled by a home brew shop

¼ cup Briess Cherrywood Smoked Malt, milled by a home brew shop

3 cups Ice Cream Base (page 34), very cold

½ cup Widmer Hefeweizen or your favorite balanced, fruity-hopped Hefeweizen, cold

In a small pot, bring 1 cup water to a boil. Reduce the heat to a lazy simmer and stir in the wheat liquid malt extract, caramel 40L malt, and cherrywood-smoked malt. Cover tightly and simmer for 30 minutes, stirring occasionally and making sure the liquid isn't boiling off.

Remove the pot from the heat and pour the syrup through a fine-mesh strainer into a small mixing bowl, pressing the hops and malt lightly to get most of the liquid out. Fill another small mixing bowl with ice, then fill it halfway with water. Set the bowl containing the syrup into the ice water and stir to quickly cool the liquid. Once the syrup is cold to the touch, use it immediately.

Put ¾ cup of the syrup, the ice cream base, and the cold beer into a bowl and whisk to combine. Pour the mixture into an ice cream maker and turn on the machine. Churn just until the mixture has the texture of soft-serve (see pages 23 to 24 for timing ranges, depending on the machine).

Transfer the ice cream, scraping every last delicious drop from the machine, into freezer-friendly containers. Cover with parchment paper, pressing it to the surface of the ice cream so it adheres, then cover with a lid. It's okay if the parchment hangs over the rim. Store it in the coldest part of your freezer (farthest from the door) until firm, at least 6 hours. It will keep for up to 3 months.

HOPPED FARMHOUSE ALE

MAKES ABOUT

2

PINTS

Long ago, farmers in northern Belgium lacked potable water to give their workers, so they brewed beer in the name of safe hydration. One of the resulting styles of these farmhouse ales is a fruity, crisp concoction with refreshing bitterness from hops and tartness from lactobacillus yeasts. Our attempt to channel these flavors brought us to The Commons Brewery in southeast Portland, makers of the exquisite Myrtle farmhouse ale, and led somehow to us making *200 gallons* of malt concentrate. This recipe calls for making your own yeasted syrup, but thank goodness, just a coffee-mug's worth. Any skeptics of scoops flavored with yeasts and hops should note that the end result kinda tastes like a more sophisticated version of old-school orange sherbet. For this recipe, you'll need an insulated coffee mug with a lid, and it would be very handy to have an instant-read thermometer.

WHAT WE LEARN: *To re-create the fermented tang of the ale, we set up a little science project. We heat a mixture of malt extract and corn syrup so it's in the right temperature range to keep lactobacillus yeast happy, eating, and replicating until we have a super-sour syrup. It starts out too sweet and over-fermented for beer but tastes like saison heaven once you churn it into ice cream. The leftover syrup keeps in the fridge for up to 1 week and makes for a funky mix for bourbon sours.*

¼ cup golden light liquid malt extract

1 tablespoon light corn syrup

2 teaspoons freshly squeezed lemon juice

2 tablespoons Omega Yeast Lactobacillus Blend

¼ cup granulated sugar

At least one day before you plan to make the ice cream, bring 1 cup water to a boil in a small saucepan, then reduce the heat to maintain a lazy simmer. Stir in the malt extract, corn syrup, and lemon juice, and keep on a low simmer. Cover tightly and cook, stirring often, for 3 minutes to fully dissolve the malt extract. Pour the mixture into a bowl. Cover the bowl with a plate and let the syrup cool until it registers 100°F to 105°F on an instant-read thermometer.

Meanwhile, clean and dry an insulated coffee mug with a tight-fitting lid. When the malt mixture reaches the right temperature, pour it into the mug, stir in the Lactobacillus Blend, and screw the lid on tight. Store the mug in a warm spot in the kitchen (like on top of the fridge) for at least 24 and up to 36 hours, occasionally giving the liquid a light swirling in the closed mug.

While waiting for the lacto syrup to ferment, we need to make a hop syrup for flavoring: Mix the sugar and ½ cup water in a small saucepan and cook over medium heat until it begins to steam. Add the hops, remove the pan from the heat, and let it sit for 20 minutes. Pour the syrup through a fine-mesh strainer (lined with a coffee filter, if using pellets) into a container and store it in the fridge until ready to use.

(recipe continues)

- **1 tablespoon** Meridian, Centennial, or other sweet, citrus-forward whole hops (or 1 teaspoon pellets)
- **3 cups** Ice Cream Base (page 34), very cold
- **2 teaspoons** finely grated grapefruit zest (use a Microplane)

Measure out ¾ cup of the lacto syrup. Chill it until it is cold, and use it within a few hours or store it in the fridge for up to 12 hours.

Put the chilled lacto syrup, ½ cup of the hop syrup, the ice cream base, and the grapefruit zest into a bowl and whisk to combine. Pour the mixture into an ice cream maker and turn on the machine. Churn just until the mixture has the texture of soft-serve (see pages 23 to 24 for timing ranges, depending on the machine).

Transfer the ice cream, scraping every last delicious drop from the machine, into freezer-friendly containers. Cover with parchment paper, pressing it to the surface of the ice cream so it adheres, then cover with a lid. It's okay if the parchment hangs over the rim. Store it in the coldest part of your freezer (farthest from the door) until firm, at least 6 hours. It will keep for up to 3 months.

HOPRICOT GELATO

Reverend Nat West might not technically be a reverend, but this local Portland character is a cider evangelist with an obsession for bygone styles and fermenting techniques. Well, we got hooked on the Rev's Hallelujah Hopricot, a heavily hopped Belgian *wit*-style cider (think coriander and orange peel) made from apples but dosed with apricots, which brings a musky tartness that pairs so well with those hops. So to celebrate his revelatory cider, we churn a gelato—with less fat and air than ice cream, it is especially dense—that features apricots and citrusy Citra hops, steeped just long enough to give us their bitter, floral yumminess but before they turn all IPA-spicy. My secret weapon is liquid champagne yeast (available at most home brew stores), which tames the sweetness and bitterness of the gelato.

⅛ ounce whole dried Cascade, Amarillo, or Citra hops

6 large apricots (a freestone variety if you can find them)

2 cups Gelato Base (page 36), very cold

1 cup heavy cream

1 teaspoon liquid champagne yeast

2 teaspoons freshly squeezed lemon juice

Bring ¾ cup water to a boil in a small saucepan, then reduce the heat to very low so the water is steaming but not bubbling. Add the hops, cover, and let steep on the heat for 15 minutes to infuse the water.

Meanwhile, cut out the pits and coarsely chop the apricots, and put them in a blender. Once the hop liquid is ready, pour it through a fine-mesh strainer into the blender, discarding the hops, and puree until smooth. Measure out 2 cups of the apricot mixture and chill in the fridge until cold. (Reserve any extra apricot puree for another purpose, like cocktails.)

In the blender, combine the gelato base, heavy cream, yeast, lemon juice, and the chilled apricot mixture and blend briefly to combine well. Pour the mixture into an ice cream maker and turn on the machine. Churn just until the mixture has the texture of a pourable frozen smoothie (see pages 23 to 24 for timing ranges, depending on the machine).

Transfer the gelato, scraping every last delicious drop from the machine, into freezer-friendly containers. Cover with parchment paper, pressing it to the surface of the gelato so it adheres, then cover with a lid. It's okay if the parchment hangs over the rim. Store it in the coldest part of your freezer (farthest from the door) until firm, at least 6 hours. It will keep for up to 3 months.

IMPERIAL STOUT MILK SORBET
WITH BLACKBERRY-FIG JAM

MAKES ABOUT
2½
PINTS

Ever since I took my first cold sip of Midnight Flight stout from Three Weavers Brewing Company, in Inglewood, California, I knew I had to try to churn my version of the creamy, dense brew with its lovely frothy head and hints of chocolate, coffee, and caramel. To help, I did something unusual: I added skim milk to a sorbet. It's a cool way to add a little body—in this case, to recoup some of the mouthfeel lost when we boil the stout—without overwhelming the delicate flavors with fat. Once it's ready, I layer in blackberry-fig jam to play up its dark, fruity notes.

WHAT WE LEARN: *Let me begin by apologizing to the fine folks at Three Weavers. After much experimenting, I decided I had to break one of my cardinal rules: I'd have to adulterate the product in order to properly feature it. So I poured their perfect stout into a pot and brought it to a boil. The step is important: For one, cooking off some of the alcohol (this stout clocks in at 9.5%) helps the ice cream freeze the way I want it to. And second, the bubbling in the pot gets rid of some of the carbon dioxide that is so welcome in the glass but would create excessive froth during the churning.*

1 bottle (330 ml) Three Weavers Imperial Stout or your favorite super-dark and malty stout

1 cup skim milk, cold

2 cups Sorbet Base (page 36), very cold

½ cup Blackberry-Fig Jam (recipe follows)

In a small pot, bring the stout to a rolling boil over medium-high heat. Then immediately remove the pot from the heat and add the milk and the sorbet base. Use a stick blender to briefly blend until well combined. Refrigerate until the mixture is cold to the touch, or up to 12 hours.

Pour the cold mixture into an ice cream maker and turn it on. Churn just until the mixture has the texture of a pourable frozen smoothie (see pages 23 to 24 for timing ranges, depending on the machine).

Stir the jam with a fork to loosen it a bit. Alternate spooning layers of the mixture and dolloping the blackberry-fig jam over each spoonful in freezer-friendly containers.

Cover with parchment paper, pressing it to the surface of the sorbet so it adheres, then cover with a lid. It's okay if the parchment hangs over the rim. Store it in the coldest part of your freezer (farthest from the door) until firm, at least 6 hours. It will keep for up to 3 months.

BLACKBERRY-FIG JAM

MAKES 2½ CUPS

⅓ cup granulated sugar

12 ounces dried Mission figs

½ cup fresh blackberries

1 teaspoon vanilla extract

Pinch kosher salt

6 tablespoons (¾ stick) unsalted butter

In a medium saucepan, combine the sugar and 2 tablespoons water. Cook over medium heat, stirring, until the sugar dissolves completely, about 2 minutes. Then, without stirring, bring the mixture to a boil and cook, swirling the pan gently if needed, until the sugar turns a light amber color. Add 1½ cups water, the dried figs, and the blackberries; the mix may sizzle and solidify. Continue to cook over medium heat until the caramel dissolves again. Reduce the heat to medium-low, cover, and cook until the fruit is soft and the liquid has reduced slightly, about 30 minutes.

Add the vanilla, salt, and butter. Transfer the jam to a food processor or blender and blend until smooth (and very thick). Let it cool to room temperature, then store in an airtight container in the fridge until cold or for up to 3 months.

CHAPTER 4

THE
FLOWER
SERIES

Spring can be a tricky season, flavor-wise. The weather says winter's done, but the farmer's market begs to differ. Sure, there may be stalks of rhubarb and a smattering of strawberries, but the full-on bounty—pallets of berries, bins of stone fruit, and tables of melons—just isn't here yet. This got me thinking about the signs of spring and how to bring the fresh feeling and bright color of the season to our menu. It got me thinking of flowers— the early, vivid signals that the gray cold of winter is truly over.

Not only do flowers symbolize this fleeting, hopeful moment, but they also present a fun challenge. Because what do flowers taste like, anyway? We explored the answer, coming at colorful blossoms from different angles. For Rose City Riot, for example, we make ice cream with rose water, which features the distilled essence of the petals, and up the flower power with cream infused with saffron, the dried stamens of a particular crocus. For other scoops, we channel the essence of wildflowers as expressed in local honey, or the nose-nipping astringent character of California poppies captured in a sweet-bitter aperitif. For a very special sorbet, we look to the perfumey sweetness of elderflower liqueur to tame the medicinal edge of dandelion-root bitters, then deck it out with a rainbow's worth of fresh edible petals. The scoops might be cold, but the bouquet of flavor is just the thing to banish any chill in the air.

WILDFLOWER HONEY
WITH RICOTTA WALNUT LACE COOKIES

MAKES ABOUT
1½
PINTS

Thanks to the beekeepers behind Bee Local, a honey-harvesting outfit based in Portland, I now know honey is all about *terroir*. The French word, which describes the connection between the places where grapes grow and the character of the wine made from them, relates just as much to the flavor of honey. As we all know, honey is made by bees from the nectar of flowers, and so its flavor depends on the particular flowers in bloom, and that in turns depends on the climate and whatever blossoms happen to be growing near the hives. Sustainably gathered and raw, Bee Local's honey reflects the place it came from, whether that's Oregon's Willamette Valley or Walla Walla, Washington. This ice cream is all about giving a platform to the punch of wildflower honeys from *your* neck of the flower patch. We heighten all that floral sweetness with lemon juice and zest. Chopped ricotta-filled lace cookies add a delicate crunch.

3 cups Ice Cream Base (page 34), very cold

½ cup fresh, soft ricotta cheese

¼ cup wildflower honey

2 tablespoons freshly squeezed lemon juice

1 tablespoon finely grated lemon zest (use a Microplane)

½ teaspoon kosher salt

1 cup chopped Ricotta Walnut Lace Cookies (recipe follows)

Put the ice cream base, ricotta, honey, lemon juice, lemon zest, and salt into a bowl and whisk to combine. Pour the mixture into an ice cream maker and turn on the machine. Churn just until the mixture has the texture of soft-serve (see pages 23 to 24 for timing ranges, depending on the machine).

Quickly transfer the ice cream into freezer-friendly containers: Spoon in a layer of ice cream, sprinkle on some of the chopped cookies, and use a spoon to press them in gently. Repeat. Cover with parchment paper, pressing it to the surface of the ice cream so it adheres, then cover with a lid. It's okay if the parchment hangs over the rim. Store it in the coldest part of your freezer (farthest from the door) until firm, at least 6 hours. It will keep for up to 3 months.

RICOTTA WALNUT LACE COOKIES

MAKES ABOUT 6 CUPS OF COOKIE PIECES

FOR THE COOKIE

1/3 cup walnut halves

4 tablespoons (1/2 stick) unsalted butter, melted

3/4 cup extra-thick rolled oats (preferably Bob's Red Mill)

1/3 cup granulated sugar

2 large eggs, lightly beaten

1 tablespoon all-purpose flour

1/2 teaspoon vanilla extract

1/2 teaspoon baking powder

1/4 teaspoon kosher salt

FOR THE ICING

8 tablespoons (1 stick) unsalted butter

2 teaspoons finely grated lemon zest (use a Microplane)

2 1/2 ounces (about 1/2 cup) requesón or queso fresco, crumbled very fine

1/2 teaspoon vanilla bean paste

Pinch kosher salt

1 3/4 cups confectioners' sugar, sifted

If you've never made delicate, crispy lace cookies, prepare for an impressive result for very little effort when a butter-forward batter of oats and ground walnuts caramelizes in the oven to become a golden-brown lattice of love. Then we slather the lattice with a lemon zest–ricotta icing. The cookies are meant for the wildflower honey ice cream, but they pair just as well with a glass of cold milk. There's enough in the recipe to enjoy them both ways!

MAKE THE COOKIE

Heat the oven to 350°F. Line a sheet pan with parchment paper, then spray the paper with nonstick cooking spray.

Use a food processor (or a very fervent knife) to chop the walnuts to a coarse powder. In a bowl, pour the melted butter over the oats and stir until combined. Add the sugar and stir until combined. Add the ground walnuts, eggs, flour, vanilla, baking powder, and salt and stir.

Pour the batter onto the parchment paper and spread it out very, very thin with a butter knife or a pastry spatula; spread it so thin that you see some gaps in the batter. Slide the cookie sheet into the oven and bake, rotating the sheet halfway through, until the cookie is fully crisped and is an amber golden brown, 12 to 15 minutes. Cool the cookie on the sheet to room temperature.

PREPARE THE ICING

In a small saucepan, heat the butter, 2 tablespoons water, and the lemon zest until the butter is completely melted. Remove the pan from the heat and whisk in half of the ricotta. Add the vanilla bean paste and the salt. Add the confectioners' sugar, about one-fourth at a time, whisking hard after each addition to work out any of the clumps. Whisk in the remaining ricotta.

Pour the icing over the cookie in one thick layer, completely coating the top. You should have a layer of icing that is about half the thickness of the cookie. If possible, put the entire sheet pan in the freezer for 1 hour in order to harden the icing (to make it easier to cut the cookie), or let it sit at room temperature for 2 hours until the icing has hardened.

Cut the cookie into small bite-size pieces (about ¼- to ½-inch) and store in the freezer until ready to use or for up to 3 months.

HONEY LAVENDER

MAKES ABOUT

2

PINTS

This might be our most divisive flavor—and for a shop that makes a flavor called Salted Caramel Thanksgiving Turkey, that's saying something. While some lavender ice creams feature the flower's brilliant purple color and a mere whiff of its bouquet, this one wallops you with it. A lick is less like strolling in a field in Provence than it is like log-rolling down a hill. For lavender lovers, this is bliss, a fragrant deep-tissue massage that culminates in a honey reiki. Use a honey that's particularly floral in flavor. We use the good stuff from Bee Local, for which honey is harvested from urban hives around Portland, and today many cities have an equivalent. Unless you're currently drying lavender at your cottage in Avignon, consider buying a bunch at the farmer's market (ask if it's pesticide-free for culinary use) or a jar at the spice shop.

$^1/_4$ cup wildflower honey

$^1/_2$ cup dried lavender (buds only)

3 cups Ice Cream Base (page 34), very cold

10 drops natural purple food coloring, preferably India Tree brand (optional)

In a small saucepan, combine ¾ cup water and the honey. Bring the mixture to a boil, stirring occasionally, then take it off the heat. Stir in the lavender, cover the saucepan, and let steep at room temperature for at least 4 hours or overnight.

Pour the syrup through a fine-mesh strainer into a container, pressing on the flower buds to extract as much liquid as possible. Chill until cold and use it right away, or refrigerate it in an airtight container for up to 2 weeks.

Put the lavender syrup, ice cream base, and food coloring (if you're using it) into a bowl and whisk to combine. Pour the mixture into an ice cream maker and turn on the machine. Churn just until the mixture has the texture of soft-serve (see pages 23 to 24 for timing ranges, depending on the machine).

Transfer the ice cream, scraping every last delicious drop from the machine, into freezer-friendly containers. Cover with parchment paper, pressing it to the surface of the ice cream so it adheres, then cover with a lid. It's okay if the parchment hangs over the rim. Store it in the coldest part of your freezer (farthest from the door) until firm, at least 6 hours. It will keep for up to 3 months.

ROSE CITY RIOT

This flavor is named for Portland but gives a nod to Iran—ice cream was more or less invented in the Middle East, after all. In particular, we celebrate the flavors of *bastani*, often referred to as "Persian ice cream." We add just enough rose water for a strolling-through-a-garden experience, rather than a drinking-from-grandma's-perfume quality. We stir in pistachios and tint the ice cream pink with beets. After we churn the ice cream, we layer it in containers with saffron-infused cream, a bastardized version of an old Persian trick of folding in frozen clotted cream that here provides a high-fat delivery system for a wallop of flower flavor.

WHAT WE LEARN: *I've made beet-flavored sorbet (see Aquabeet Sorbet, page 158), but more often, I use beets not for their flavor but for their stunning red color. You should, too! Store extra beet syrup in an ice cube tray until frozen, then transfer the cubes to self-seal bags and freeze them for up to 4 months. Thaw a few whenever you want to turn cakes, cocktails, or buttercream pink.*

½ cup granulated sugar

¼ cup coarsely shredded peeled red beets

3 cups Ice Cream Base (page 34), very cold

4 teaspoons rose water

⅓ cup unsalted roasted pistachios, coarsely chopped

⅓ cup Saffron Cream (recipe follows)

Combine the sugar, ½ cup water, and the shredded beets in a small saucepan, set it over medium heat, and let it come to a simmer. Reduce the heat to maintain a bare simmer and cook for 5 minutes. Strain the beets through a fine-mesh strainer into a heatproof container; discard the solids. Let the syrup cool completely, then cover and refrigerate until it's cold to the touch. Use right away or freeze in ice cube trays (then in bags) for up to 4 months.

Put the ice cream base, rose water, and 2 tablespoons of the beet syrup into a bowl and whisk to combine. Pour the mixture into an ice cream maker and turn on the machine. Churn just until the mixture has the texture of soft-serve (see pages 23 to 24 for timing ranges, depending on the machine).

Quickly transfer the ice cream into freezer-friendly containers: Spoon in a layer of ice cream, sprinkle on some of the pistachios, and use a spoon to press them in gently. Drizzle in just enough saffron cream to make a very thin layer. Repeat.

Cover with parchment paper, pressing it to the surface of the ice cream so it adheres, then cover with a lid. It's okay if the parchment hangs over the rim. Store it in the coldest part of your freezer (farthest from the door) until firm, at least 6 hours. It will keep for up to 3 months.

SAFFRON CREAM

MAKES ABOUT 1 CUP

1 cup heavy cream
5 saffron threads

Pour the cream into a small saucepan, crumble in the saffron, and bring it to a simmer over medium heat (be careful not to let it boil). Let it simmer, stirring it occasionally, for about 5 minutes. Then remove the pan from the heat and let the cream cool to room temperature. Transfer it to an airtight container and refrigerate until cold or for up to 1 week.

GRAND POPPY-SEED SHERBET

MAKES ABOUT

3

PINTS

A frolic in a California meadow distilled in a scoop, this pale orange sherbet is made with one of my pet products: Grand Poppy organic liqueur from Greenbar Distillery. Greenbar is cool for a million reasons—they're the first distillery established in L.A. since Prohibition ended, they source ingredients within 100 miles of L.A., and they plant a tree for every bottle sold—but number one on my list is still this aperitif-style liqueur packed with SoCal citrus, coastal herbs, and of course the California poppy. Other bitter, floral liqueurs work well in this sherbet—try the gentian root–based Suze or Salers; bitter, aromatic Amaros like Fernet; and citrusy Bigallet's China-China Amer.

WHAT WE LEARN: *Because the aromas of these spirits just can't come through on their own in the frozen treat, we look to swirls of lemony homemade marshmallow fluff (sugar aerated with egg whites—essentially marshmallow minus gelatin) to mimic the sensation. Since it melts fast and is packed with citrus zest, the fluff hits your nose quickly and you experience it as fragrance as well as flavor. Try it with other ingredients whose aroma would be a shame to sacrifice, like maple (see page 202).*

2 cups Sorbet Base
(page 36), very
cold

³/₄ cup whole milk

¹/₂ cup heavy cream

¹/₄ cup Grand Poppy
liqueur or another
floral aperitif,
very cold

¹/₄ cup freshly
squeezed lemon
juice, very cold

1 teaspoon vanilla
extract, preferably
Tahitian

1 tablespoon finely
grated lemon zest
(use a Microplane)

2 teaspoons poppy
seeds

1 cup Lemon
Marshmallow Fluff
(recipe follows)

Put the sorbet base, milk, cream, liqueur, lemon juice, vanilla, and lemon zest into a bowl and use a stick blender to briefly blend until well combined. Stir in the poppy seeds. Pour the mixture into an ice cream maker and turn on the machine. Churn just until the mixture has the texture of a pourable frozen smoothie (see pages 23 to 24 for timing ranges, depending on the machine).

Alternate spooning layers of the mixture and generous dollops of fluff in freezer-friendly containers.

Cover with parchment paper, pressing it to the surface of the sherbet so it adheres, then cover with a lid. It's okay if the parchment hangs over the rim. Store it in the coldest part of your freezer (farthest from the door) until firm, at least 6 hours. It will keep for up to 3 months.

LEMON MARSHMALLOW FLUFF

MAKES ABOUT 6 CUPS

3 large egg whites (without even a speck of yolk!)

$\frac{1}{2}$ teaspoon cream of tartar

$\frac{2}{3}$ cup light corn syrup

$\frac{1}{4}$ cup granulated sugar

1 tablespoon finely grated lemon zest (use a Microplane)

In a stand mixer fitted with the whisk attachment, beat the egg whites on medium-high speed just until they look frothy. Add the cream of tartar and continue to beat until the whites reach soft peak stage, 2 to 3 minutes. Reduce the mixer speed to the lowest setting and let that run while you make the sugar syrup.

Mix the corn syrup, sugar, and ¼ cup water in a medium saucepan and attach the candy thermometer to the pan. Cook on medium-high heat, stirring constantly, until the syrup goes from cloudy to clear. Stop stirring and continue heating on medium-high until the syrup reaches 238°F. Immediately remove the pan from the heat, raise the mixer speed to medium-low, and drizzle the hot sugar syrup into the mixer in a thin, steady stream, aiming for the hot sugar to hit only the egg whites and not the bowl.

Once the syrup is well combined, raise the speed to medium-high and beat until the mixture looks glossy and has cooled until it is warm to the touch, 2 to 3 minutes. Add the lemon zest and beat just until the zest is well combined, about 1 minute. Transfer the fluff to a container and then use it immediately or cover and refrigerate it for up to 1 week.

NOTE

*My favorite flowers
for this are pansies
and borage because
they're peppery
and juicy, but also
because they can go
right into the sorbet
with just a brief wash.
For other tasty types,
like those begonias,
roses, nasturtiums,
marigolds,
chrysanthemums,
and apple blossoms,
you'll have to pluck
individual petals and
remove the pistils.
Keep in mind that to
avoid a mouthful of
pesticides, you should
only use flowers that
grow wild or ask if the
flowers you're about
to buy are okay for
eating.*

DANDELION BITTERS SORBET
WITH EDIBLE FLOWERS

MAKES ABOUT

2

PINTS

Talk about flower power! First we churn a pale yellow sorbet made with elderflower, whose flavor is like a pear-lychee mash-up, and dandelion bitters, which plays tug-of-war with that classy floral sweetness. Then we go wild, suspending edible flowers of all colors in frozen glory. While we pluck spring's first buds from Viridian Farms in Oregon's Willamette Valley, you should raid your garden—you do have a garden brimming with borage and begonias, don't you?—or find a farmer in your area and start chatting about what she grows that you can eat.

2 cups Sorbet Base (page 36), very cold

¼ cup elderflower syrup (I like the Nikolaihof brand)

2 tablespoons freshly squeezed lemon juice

1 tablespoon dandelion root bitters (I like Dr. Adam Elmegirab's Dandelion & Burdock Bitters)

About 30 edible flowers (see Note)

Put the sorbet base, 1½ cups water, elderflower syrup, lemon juice, and dandelion bitters into a bowl and use a stick blender to briefly blend until well combined. Pour the mixture into an ice cream maker and turn on the machine. Churn just until the mixture has the texture of a pourable frozen smoothie (see pages 23 to 24 for timing ranges, depending on the machine).

Alternate spooning the mixture and adding a single layer of flowers in freezer-friendly containers.

Cover with parchment paper, pressing it to the surface of the ice cream so it adheres, then cover with a lid. It's okay if the parchment hangs over the rim. Store it in the coldest part of your freezer (farthest from the door) until firm, at least 6 hours. It will keep for up to 3 months.

CHAPTER 5

THE BERRY SERIES

Where we live, July is the time when the farmer's market is flooded with our annual berry bounty. We go all in for the month, devoting our entire menu to the gorgeous orbs and clusters. The pea-size wild blueberries that surround mountain hikers. The delicate marionberries—a blackberry hybrid with a cult following—from Marion County, in Oregon's Willamette Valley. The famous Hood strawberries, a variety so intensely flavorful and juicy that they make otherwise yummy varieties taste like duds.

This focus gives us a chance to acknowledge a crucial, delicious moment in agricultural history. In the nineteenth century, settlers in the Oregon Territory planted orchards of hardy fruits like apples and pears. Yet because those trees can take five years or more to bear fruit, they also propagated berry plants, which take far less time, and they then feasted on the blue, purple, and red rewards. Now berries are big business here, fueling the local economy and delighting the denizens of Portlandia, because we grow—if you'll forgive me a proud-papa moment—some of the best in the world.

An all-berry menu also gives us an opportunity to let customers taste flavors side by side, a fun way to showcase the particular pleasures of each berry and the intention that goes into each creation. Briefly roasted to intensify their flavor, strawberries become sorbet, delivering flavor fast and furiously onto your tongue before it leaves without a trace, mimicking the juicy punch of a ripe strawberry eaten out of hand. We apply a judicious amount of fat to wild lingon-, huckle-, and blackberries to create a sherbet that lets their flavor and dusky tartness linger a little on your tongue. When we do want the lushness of proper ice cream, we transform berries into jams, condensing their flavors so they don't get lost in that lovely fat.

When you set out to make these, embrace your inner berry snob and ditch the supermarket for the folding tables of a farm stand or the DIY fun of the nearest U-Pick. Then prepare for some purple-fingered, counter-staining fun.

MEYER LEMON BLUEBERRY BUTTERMILK CUSTARD

Oh California, paradise of produce, land of the Meyer lemon, a smooth-skinned fruit with a milder acidity and more complex flavor than the everyday lemon. In our L.A. kitchen, a glut of citrus inspired us to devise an ice cream that's both super bright and super rich. The tang of lemon and buttermilk sets the stage for dense, egg yolk–fortified ice cream and sweet blueberry jam that's swirled in to keep the push-pull of flavors going. If you can't get Meyer lemons, this is still super yummy with regular ones.

WHAT WE LEARN: *Only rarely at Salt & Straw do we use a custard base, a concoction of egg yolks and dairy that spins to a particularly creamy texture. The yolks do a few things here: chief among them, they add flavor and they act as an emulsifier so that you can exceed the upper limit of butterfat in your ice cream, which maxes out at 18% with dairy alone. The yolks let you make an over-the-top ice cream without literally churning butter. And our custard base is actually much easier to make than traditional ones that call for you to boil the dairy, carefully whisk it into the eggs without cooking them, then slowly cook the mixture while stirring so you don't scramble the eggs. In ours, you just heat the dairy, whisk it into the eggs, and you're done. FYI: The eggs don't get fully cooked, so beware if you're not into that sort of thing.*

FOR THE BUTTERMILK CUSTARD BASE

- ½ cup plus 2 tablespoons granulated sugar
- 2 tablespoons dry milk powder
- ¼ teaspoon xanthan gum (Yes, I'm easy to find! See page 33.)
- 4 large egg yolks
- 2 tablespoons light corn syrup
- 1½ cups heavy cream
- 1½ cups buttermilk

MAKE THE BASE

Combine the ½ cup sugar, the dry milk powder, and the xanthan gum in a small bowl and stir well. In a large bowl, combine the egg yolks and the remaining 2 tablespoons sugar and whisk until the yolks are lighter in color, about 1 minute.

In a medium pot, combine the corn syrup and the cream. Add the sugar mixture and immediately whisk vigorously until smooth. Set the pot over medium heat and cook, stirring often and adjusting the heat if necessary to prevent a simmer, until the sugar has fully dissolved, about 3 minutes. Remove the pot from the heat. Start whisking the yolk mixture and continue to whisk constantly while slowly drizzling the hot cream into the yolks.

(recipe continues)

Add the buttermilk and whisk until fully combined. Transfer the base to an airtight container and refrigerate until well chilled, at least 6 hours, or for even better texture and flavor, 24 hours. It can be further stored in the fridge for up to 1 week or in the freezer for up to 3 months.

FOR THE LEMON BLUEBERRY ICE CREAM

Grated zest (use a Microplane) and juice of 1 Meyer lemon

¼ teaspoon kosher salt

½ cup Blueberry Jam (recipe follows), or ½ cup store-bought jam mixed with freshly squeezed lemon juice to taste

MAKE THE ICE CREAM

In a bowl, combine the (very cold) buttermilk custard base, lemon zest and juice, and salt and whisk to get the lemon fully incorporated. Pour the mixture into an ice cream maker and turn on the machine. Churn just until the mixture has the texture of soft-serve (see pages 23 to 24 for timing ranges, depending on the machine).

Stir the jam with a fork to loosen it. Alternate spooning layers of the custard and dolloping blueberry jam over each spoonful in freezer-friendly containers.

Cover with parchment paper, pressing it to the surface of the ice cream so it adheres, then cover with a lid. It's okay if the parchment hangs over the rim. Store it in the coldest part of your freezer (farthest from the door) until firm, at least 6 hours. It will keep for up to 3 months.

BLUEBERRY JAM

MAKES ABOUT 2 CUPS

1 pint fresh blueberries

2 tablespoons freshly squeezed lemon juice

1 tablespoon pectin

1 cup granulated sugar

In a food processor, puree the blueberries. In a medium pot, heat the blueberry puree, lemon juice, and pectin over medium-high heat, stirring constantly, until it reaches a boil. Stir in the sugar and continue to cook over medium-high heat until the mixture comes back to a boil. Immediately remove the pot from the heat and let the jam cool to room temperature. Chill the jam thoroughly before using. It can be stored in the fridge for up to 3 months.

BLACK RASPBERRY COBBLER FRO-YO

MAKES ABOUT
3
PINTS

Frozen yogurt makes a great backdrop for sweet-tart fruit, like the winy black raspberries we make into a simple jam. (Of course, any tasty purchased jam will do. If it's especially seedy, consider passing half of it through a medium-mesh sieve to remove some of the grit.) A sort-of-classic streusel adds some welcome sweetness and takes on the crunch of roasted nuts when frozen. I say "sort-of-classic" because we use a little masa harina (dried nixtamalized corn, the same stuff that's used to make tortillas) with the flour, just enough to give the streusel an unexpected flavor.

WHAT WE LEARN: *Fro-yo has had several lives—as an ostensibly healthier alternative to ice cream and as a self-serve unlimited-toppings fad. But frozen yogurt done well stands on its own merits. The relatively low-fat content gives it a dense sherbet-like texture, and without the airiness of ice cream, it brings on the milky tang. You can churn the same mixture of sorbet base and yogurt described here, then flavor it however you want—whether that's with an infusion into the yogurt, homemade jam, or gummy bears.*

½ cup store-bought
   black raspberry
   jam

1 teaspoon freshly
   squeezed lemon
   juice

1½ cups Sorbet Base
   (page 36), very
   cold

1½ cups super-tart
   Greek yogurt (I
   like the Ellenos
   or Straus brands),
   very cold

¾ cup whole milk

¼ teaspoon kosher
   salt

½ cup Masa Streusel
   (recipe follows)

In a bowl, mix the jam and lemon juice until well combined. Set it aside.

Put the sorbet base, yogurt, milk, and salt into a bowl and use a stick blender to briefly blend until well combined. Pour the mixture into an ice cream maker and turn on the machine. Churn just until the mixture has the texture of a pourable frozen smoothie (see pages 23 to 24 for timing ranges, depending on the machine).

Quickly transfer the fro-yo into freezer-friendly containers: Spoon in layers of fro-yo, sprinkles of the streusel, using a spoon to press them in gently, and dollops of jam.

Cover with parchment paper, pressing it to the surface of the fro-yo so it adheres, then cover with a lid. It's okay if the parchment hangs over the rim. Store it in the coldest part of your freezer (farthest from the door) until firm, at least 6 hours. It will keep for up to 3 months.

MASA STREUSEL

MAKES ABOUT 2 CUPS OF YUMMY CRUMBLE

½ cup granulated sugar

½ cup masa harina

¼ cup all-purpose flour

¼ teaspoon ground cinnamon

¼ teaspoon kosher salt

4 tablespoons (½ stick) cold unsalted butter, cut into pea-size cubes

¼ teaspoon vanilla extract, preferably Mexican

Heat the oven to 350°F and line a sheet pan with parchment paper.

In a bowl, combine the sugar, masa, flour, cinnamon, and salt. Add the butter and vanilla, and use the back of a fork to mix the crumble until it forms fine, pea-size crumbs.

Sprinkle the crumble on the prepared sheet pan to form a ¼-inch-thick layer, then lightly press down on the crumble so it sticks together a bit. Bake the crumble until it is light golden brown, about 15 minutes. Let it cool to room temperature, then break it up into pea-size pieces. Use immediately or store in an airtight container at room temperature for up to 2 weeks.

GOAT CHEESE MARIONBERRY HABANERO

MAKES ABOUT
2½
PINTS

We love Portland Creamery's Sweet Fire chevre so much that we devoted a flavor to it. Cheesemaker Liz Alvis tops her creamy, tangy triumph—from a herd of free-roaming goats in Molalla, Oregon—with syrup made from habanero chiles and the blackberry cousins called marionberries. To celebrate every rich, fiery bite, we make ice cream from her exceptional cheese and add streaks of marionberry jam infused with the floral, hot-hot-hot chile. Your favorite goat cheese will fit the bill and so will seedless blackberry or black raspberry jam, if you can't get your hands on marionberry. The amount of chile is up to you, too, though remember that the bigger the wallop of spiciness, the sweeter the next lick of cold cream.

3 cups Ice Cream Base (page 34), very cold

6 ounces (⅔ cup) fresh goat cheese, at room temperature

½ teaspoon kosher salt

1 teaspoon freshly squeezed lemon juice

½ cup Marionberry-Habanero Jam (recipe follows)

Combine the ice cream base, goat cheese, and salt in a bowl and use a stick blender to completely incorporate the cheese. If you're using a frozen-bowl type of machine, cover and chill in the fridge until cold. Stir in the lemon juice, then immediately pour the mixture into an ice cream maker and turn on the machine. Churn just until the mixture has the texture of soft-serve (see pages 23 to 24 for timing ranges, depending on the machine).

Stir the jam with a fork to loosen it. Alternate spooning layers of the mixture and generous dollops of jam in freezer-friendly containers.

Cover with parchment paper, pressing it to the surface of the ice cream so it adheres, then cover with a lid. It's okay if the parchment hangs over the rim. Store it in the coldest part of your freezer (farthest from the door) until firm, at least 6 hours. It will keep for up to 3 months.

MARIONBERRY-HABANERO JAM

MAKES ABOUT ¾ CUP

One 11-ounce jar seedless marionberry, seedless blackberry, or seedless black raspberry jam

1 fresh habanero chile, coarsely chopped, seeds removed if you prefer less heat

Combine ¼ cup of the jam and the habanero in a small saucepan. Cook over medium-low heat, stirring the mixture occasionally, until the jam liquefies and just begins to simmer, about 5 minutes.

Strain the mixture through a fine-mesh strainer into a bowl, then add the remaining jam and stir well to combine. Refrigerate until fully chilled. Stored in a glass jar with a tight-fitting lid, the jam will keep in the fridge for up to 6 months.

FORAGED-BERRY SHERBET

MAKES ABOUT
2½
PINTS

To celebrate the wild harvest from the bushes and brambles of Oregon and Washington, we first think berries and then we think fat. For the fruit, we teamed up with Tom LaMonte, forager-in-chief at Northwest Wild Foods, whose small army of gatherers roam local slopes looking for the tiny, intense huckleberries, lingonberries, and other wild beauties that make this flavor so special; at home, use the most fragrant berries you can find. Ingredients this precious deserve just a touch of fat, so the extraordinary flavor lingers on your tongue.

WHAT WE LEARN: *The judicious use of fat can carry berry flavor without trampling it, especially if you can boost some of the qualities of the berries. Sugar helps, and so does acidity. Having a variety of acids at your disposal is an amazing tool. To maximize the berry-ness, here we look to a really cool ingredient called malic acid, extracted from fruits like blackberries and blueberries to provide a complementary kind of tang. In case you're tempted to say acid is acid, try making your next batch of guacamole with cider vinegar instead of lime. Or, in other words, don't!*

1 pint (12 ounces)
super-ripe mixed
berries (you can
sub frozen mixed
huckleberries and
blueberries)

½ cup boiling water

½ teaspoon
malic acid or
1 tablespoon
freshly squeezed
lemon juice

¼ teaspoon kosher
salt

2 cups Sorbet Base
(page 36), very
cold

½ cup heavy cream

Put the berries in a blender and add the boiling water, malic acid, and salt. Blend until the mixture is as smooth as possible. Refrigerate (blender jar and all) until cold.

Add the sorbet base and cream to the blender and briefly blend to combine well. Pour the mixture into an ice cream maker and turn on the machine. Churn just until the mixture has the texture of a pourable frozen smoothie (see pages 23 to 24 for timing ranges, depending on the machine).

Transfer the sherbet, scraping every last delicious drop from the machine, into freezer-friendly containers. Cover with parchment paper, pressing it to the surface of the sherbet so it adheres, then cover with a lid. It's okay if the parchment hangs over the rim. Store it in the coldest part of your freezer (farthest from the door) until firm, at least 6 hours. It will keep for up to 3 months.

STRAWBERRY-CILANTRO SORBET

MAKES ABOUT
2
PINTS

Top-notch strawberries don't need much help to make top-notch sorbet. Then again, vanilla ice cream doesn't technically *need* chips, cookies, or hot fudge. Since I'm in the business of wants, not needs, I embraced the chance to experiment with the sublime flavor essences crafted by San Francisco perfumist extraordinaire Mandy Aftel. (Her other fans include certified chef-geniuses Wylie Dufresne and Daniel Patterson.) Just a few drops of Mandy's cilantro (or as she calls it, coriander leaf) essence gives the concentrated strawberry flavor a surprising lift.

1 pint (12 ounces) super-ripe fresh strawberries, washed and hulled

1/4 cup granulated sugar

1/4 teaspoon kosher salt

1/4 teaspoon malic acid or 2 teaspoons freshly squeezed lemon juice

2 cups Sorbet Base (page 36), very cold

4 drops Coriander Leaf Chef's Essence (from aftelier.com)

Heat the oven to 350°F.

Put the berries in a small baking dish and toss them with the sugar and salt. Bake, without stirring, until the berries concentrate in flavor but have not yet begun to caramelize, about 20 minutes. Let the berries cool to room temperature.

Transfer the berries (and any juices) to a blender, add the malic acid, and blend until smooth. Transfer the puree to a bowl. Refrigerate until cold, and use immediately or keep for up to 3 days.

Measure 1 cup of the puree (reserve any extra for another purpose, like topping another ice cream). Combine the puree in the blender with the sorbet base, 1 cup water, and the coriander leaf essence, and briefly blend until well combined. Pour the mixture into an ice cream machine and turn it on. Churn just until the mixture has the texture of a pourable frozen smoothie (see pages 23 to 24 for timing ranges, depending on the machine).

Transfer the sorbet, scraping every last delicious drop from the machine, into freezer-friendly containers. Cover with parchment paper, pressing it to the surface of the sorbet so it adheres, then cover with a lid. It's okay if the parchment hangs over the rim. Store it in the coldest part of your freezer (farthest from the door) until firm, at least 6 hours. It will keep for up to 3 months.

CHAPTER 6

THE FARMER'S MARKET SERIES

In the early days of Salt & Straw, I dreamed of making "farm-to-cone" ice cream. You know, a farmer drives up to our back door, delivers her gemlike strawberries or just-picked peaches, then I lovingly churn them into scoopable bliss. But I've since realized that I just can't resist *any* of the stunning produce I see at the farmer's markets, especially in that fleeting moment when summer's and fall's bounties converge.

So instead of focusing only on the peaches, watermelons, and other usual suspects, I have fun exploring vegetables that all of us unjustly slot into the savory category. Corn and beets are obvious passengers for a journey on the sweet side, but cauliflower and parsnips, roasted to caramelize their natural sugars and draw out their complex flavors, are surprise voyagers that make indisputable sense at first lick. While the recipes in this chapter shouldn't be mistaken as novelty for novelty's sake, I do like the way double-take-inducing flavors draw people's attention and provoke conversation.

CARAMEL CORN ON THE COB

MAKES ABOUT
2
PINTS

Long before every pastry chef worth his or her salt was sprinkling, well, salt on toffees, cakes, and custards, caramel corn cornered the market for sophisticated snackery. Caramel-coated popcorn began its ascent at the 1893 World's Fair, when a Cracker Jack prototype set off a wave of deliciousness that reached carnivals throughout the country. In our rendition, we swap out exploded dried kernels for candy-sweet fresh corn, using its flavor's association with dinner, rather than dessert, to both provoke and delight.

2 tablespoons
  unsalted butter

1 cup raw corn
  kernels, freshly
  sliced off the ear
  (from 1 to
  2 ears of corn)

3/4 cup whole milk

2 tablespoons
  granulated sugar

1/2 teaspoon kosher
  salt

3 cups Ice Cream
  Base (page 34),
  very cold

1/2 cup Vanilla
  Caramel (recipe
  follows)

In a small pot, cook the butter over medium heat, stirring it occasionally with a spatula, until it begins to turn a golden amber color and smells nutty, 3 to 5 minutes. Add the corn kernels and cook, stirring frequently, until they begin to soften, about 1 minute. Add the milk, sugar, and salt, and raise the heat to high and bring to a boil. Cover the pot, reduce the heat to cook at a lazy simmer, and cook for 25 minutes, stirring every 5 minutes or so.

Strain the mixture through a fine-mesh strainer into a container, pressing on the corn to extract as much liquid as possible. Discard the corn. Let the liquid cool to room temperature, then chill until cold, or up to 5 days. Before using, scrape any solidified butter off the top.

Put the ice cream base and the corn flavoring into a bowl and whisk to combine. Pour the mixture into an ice cream maker and turn on the machine. Churn just until the mixture has the texture of soft-serve (see pages 23 to 24 for timing ranges, depending on the machine).

Alternate spooning layers of the mixture and thick swirls of vanilla caramel in freezer-friendly containers.

Cover with parchment paper, pressing it to the surface of the ice cream so it adheres, then cover with a lid. It's okay if the parchment hangs over the rim. Store it in the coldest part of your freezer (farthest from the door) until firm, at least 6 hours. It will keep for up to 3 months.

VANILLA CARAMEL

MAKES ABOUT 2 CUPS

1½ cups granulated sugar

¼ cup light corn syrup

1¼ cups heavy cream

2 tablespoons cold unsalted butter, cut into several pieces

½ teaspoon kosher salt

½ teaspoon vanilla bean paste

Combine the sugar, corn syrup, and ¼ cup water in a medium saucepan, and stir until all of the sugar looks wet. Cover, set the pan over medium-high heat, and cook, stirring occasionally, until the sugar has completely melted, about 3 minutes.

Continue to cook, covered but this time without stirring, until the mixture has thickened slightly, about 3 minutes. Remove the lid and continue cooking, without stirring but paying close attention, until the mixture is the color of light maple syrup, about 2 minutes more.

Take the pan off the heat, and immediately stand back and pour in the cream in a nice steady stream (whatever you do, do not dump it all in at once!), stirring as you pour. It'll bubble furiously.

Put the pan over medium-high heat again. Attach a candy thermometer to the side of the pan. Let the mixture simmer away, stirring it occasionally, until it registers 230°F on the thermometer, about 5 minutes. Take the pan off the heat and add the butter, salt, and vanilla bean paste, stirring slowly but constantly until the butter has completely melted.

Let the caramel cool to room temperature, and chill it in the fridge if using a frozen-bowl type of machine. Store it in an airtight container at room temperature for up to 2 weeks or in the refrigerator for up to 3 months. Separation is totally normal; just make sure to stir it well before using.

CAULIFLOWER GARAM MASALA

MAKES ABOUT

2½

PINTS

I adore spice blends that tread the line between sweet and savory. Of course, as an ice cream person, I particularly love to explore the sweet side. So I made a version of garam masala, the Indian spice blend, that is highly inauthentic but really, really good in ice cream. The particular combination of cinnamon, cardamom, Cubeb pepper, and caraway creates a thrilling *Fight Club* of flavor, each one scrapping for the attention of your tongue. To showcase the fun, I decided on sweet dark-roasted cauliflower, which is just mild-mannered enough to stay in the background and has just enough muskiness for those spices to grab on to. Unlikely as it seems, this ice cream has become one of our most popular, turning dowdy cauliflower into a spicy vegetable vixen.

1 medium head cauliflower (1⅓ pounds), leaves removed and base trimmed

4 tablespoons unsalted butter, melted

1 teaspoon kosher salt

2 teaspoons Sweet Garam Masala (recipe follows; or use store-bought and add a hefty pinch of cinnamon to sweeten it up)

¼ cup whole milk

1 tablespoon freshly squeezed lemon juice

3 cups Ice Cream Base (page 34), very cold

Heat the oven to 350°F.

Slice the cauliflower into four ½-inch-thick slabs, cutting across the stem. Put the cauliflower on a small sheet pan, drizzle with the melted butter, sprinkle with ¼ teaspoon of the salt, and toss to coat. Spread the cauliflower in a single layer, sprinkle on the garam masala, and roast, without stirring, until the florets are super tender and a beautiful golden color on the bottoms, about 30 minutes.

Roughly chop the roasted cauliflower and measure 1 packed cup (eat the rest) into a blender. In a small pot or a microwave, heat the milk until it's just hot to the touch. Add the hot milk, lemon juice, and the remaining ¾ teaspoon salt to the cauliflower and puree until it's completely smooth (see Note, page 152). Pass the puree through a fine-mesh strainer (or a *tamis* if you have one) into a container, pushing on the puree with the back of a spoon to extract as much as possible. Use immediately (chill until cold if using a frozen-bowl type of machine) or store in the refrigerator for up to 3 days.

Put the ice cream base and ¾ cup cauliflower puree into a bowl and whisk to combine. Pour the mixture into an ice cream maker and turn on the machine. Churn just until the mixture has the texture of soft-serve (see pages 23 to 24 for timing ranges, depending on the machine).

Transfer the ice cream, scraping every last delicious drop from the machine, into freezer-friendly containers. Cover with parchment paper, pressing it to the surface of the ice cream so it adheres, then cover with a lid. It's okay if the parchment hangs over the rim. Store it in the coldest part of your freezer (farthest from the door) until firm, at least 6 hours. It will keep for up to 3 months.

NOTE

To get a silky-smooth
cauliflower puree, the
best tool out there is
a fine-mesh tamis, a
drum-shaped sieve.
Once you buy one,
you'll find all sorts
of other uses for it,
from sifting your
home-ground spice
blends to removing
lumps from batters.
But sure, a fine-mesh
strainer will do the
trick as well.

SWEET GARAM MASALA

MAKES ABOUT ½ CUP

1½ tablespoons green cardamom pods

1 large black cardamom pod

1¾ teaspoons Cubeb or standard black peppercorns

½ teaspoon caraway seeds

1 teaspoon whole cloves

2 bay leaves

⅓ cup (lightly packed) ground cinnamon

1 tablespoon freshly grated nutmeg

Pinch ground mace

Ditch any dusty jarred powders for this ice cream and try toasting and grinding the spices yourself. It makes the flavors a thousand times better.

Heat the oven to 325°F.

Whack the green and black cardamom pods with the flat part of a chef's knife. Reserve the seeds and discard the pods.

Put the cardamom seeds, peppercorns, caraway, cloves, and bay leaves on a small sheet pan and toast in the oven, stirring them occasionally, until the entire kitchen smells incredible, about 4 minutes. Use a spice grinder to grind the toasted spices to a fine powder. Then transfer the mixture to a medium-mesh strainer set over a bowl and sift to remove any remaining chunks; discard the chunks. Stir in the cinnamon, nutmeg, and mace. Keep in an airtight container at room temperature for up to 6 weeks.

GREEN APPLE & MAYO SHERBET

Okay, I know what you're thinking: *Mayo in ice cream? What's wrong with this guy?* Plenty! But not because I made ice cream with a little fat, egg, and acidity—that's what mayonnaise is, after all. Including this emulsion—two antagonistic liquids bound together by science—lets you churn a textural marvel: a tart green apple sherbet with the density of sorbet and the creaminess of gelato. If I didn't totally troll you with the title, you'd have no clue about the secret ingredient.

3 large tart green
  apples, such as
  Granny Smith,
  unpeeled

1 tablespoon freshly
  squeezed lemon
  juice

½ teaspoon malic
  acid or another
  1 tablespoon lemon
  juice

2 cups Sorbet Base
  (page 36), very
  cold

½ cup heavy cream

½ cup Ice Cream
  Mayonnaise (recipe
  follows); or use
  Vegenaise (It's
  amazing!)

Core and coarsely chop the apples. Put the apples, the 1 tablespoon lemon juice, and the malic acid in a blender and blend until smooth. Strain the puree through a fine-mesh sieve into a measuring cup, pressing and stirring to extract as much liquid as you can. Measure out 1 cup of the juice (drink any extra).

Pour the 1 cup of strained apple juice back in the blender. Add the sorbet base, cream, and mayonnaise, and briefly blend to combine well. Chill it until cold if you are using a frozen-bowl type of machine. Pour the mixture into an ice cream maker and turn on the machine. Churn just until the mixture has the texture of a pourable frozen smoothie (see pages 23 to 24 for timing ranges, depending on the machine).

Transfer the sherbet into freezer-friendly containers, scraping every last delicious drop from the machine. Cover with parchment paper, pressing it to the surface of the sherbet so it adheres, then cover with a lid. It's okay if the parchment hangs over the rim. Store it in the coldest part of your freezer (farthest from the door) until firm, at least 6 hours. It will keep for up to 3 months.

ICE CREAM MAYONNAISE

MAKES ABOUT 1 CUP

2/3 cup grassy, peppery olive oil, such as Arbequina

2 tablespoons apple cider vinegar

1 tablespoon granulated sugar

1/8 teaspoon kosher salt

2 large egg yolks, lightly beaten

Leftovers of this tangy, loose mayo make a mean dressing for a pseudo-Waldorf salad with chopped walnuts, apples, celery, and grapes.

Combine the olive oil, vinegar, sugar, salt, and egg yolks in a small mixing bowl. Use a stick blender to blend until smooth and creamy, like runny mayonnaise. Use it right away or refrigerate it in an airtight container for up to 1 week.

ROASTED PARSNIP & BANANA SORBET

Parsnips and bananas might seem like an odd couple, but believe me, the combo of sweet root vegetable and tree fruit is love at first bite. In fact, the two have more in common than you'd think. Back in World War II–era England, savvy cooks frustrated by a dearth of bananas made "mock bananas" out of—you guessed it—parsnips, cooking them to custard-like softness and concentrating their very-similar-if-you-think-about-it sweetness. We roast them both and churn them into a rich sorbet, their sweetness naturally tinged with notes of warm spices that we nudge forward with a little clove and cinnamon.

1 overripe banana
  (I mean super
  black)

2 medium parsnips,
  cut into $1/4$-inch-
  thick medallions
  ($3/4$ cup)

1 tablespoon coconut
  oil, melted

1 tablespoon freshly
  squeezed lemon
  juice

2 teaspoons bourbon

$1/2$ teaspoon vanilla
  extract

Pinch kosher salt

2 pinches ground
  cinnamon

Pinch ground cloves

$1^3/4$ cups Sorbet Base
  (page 36), very
  cold

Heat the oven to 350°F.

Cut off the very top and bottom of the banana and peel it, saving the peel. Cut half the banana into ¼-inch-thick medallions and put them into a small baking dish (you can use the rest for smoothies or banana pudding). Add the parsnips to the baking dish. Pour the melted coconut oil over the bananas and parsnips and cover them with the reserved banana peel, outside facing up. Bake in the oven until the parsnips are completely tender, 15 to 20 minutes.

Remove the baking dish from the oven, throw out the burnt banana skin, and transfer the roasted bananas and parsnips to a blender. Add 1¼ cups water and the lemon juice, bourbon, vanilla, salt, cinnamon, and cloves. Blend until completely smooth, about 2 minutes. Pour the mixture into a container, cover with plastic wrap pressed onto the surface, and let it cool to room temperature.

Combine the sorbet base in a blender with the banana-parsnip puree and briefly blend until well combined. If you are using a frozen-bowl type of machine, chill the mixture in the fridge with its surface again covered with plastic wrap. Pour the mixture into an ice cream maker and turn on the machine. Churn just until the mixture has the texture of a pourable frozen smoothie (see pages 23 to 24 for timing ranges, depending on the machine).

Transfer the sorbet, scraping every last delicious drop from the machine, into freezer-friendly containers. Cover with parchment paper, pressing it to the surface of the sorbet so it adheres, then cover with a lid. It's okay if the parchment hangs over the rim. Store it in the coldest part of your freezer (farthest from the door) until firm, at least 6 hours. It will keep for up to 3 months.

AQUABEET SORBET

MAKES ABOUT
2
PINTS

Portland chef-genius Gabe Rucker once told me that puns make for the best flavors. I thought he was joking. Then I tasted Krogstad aquavit, made by House Spirits Distillery in Portland. I fell in love with the way it features the flavors of caraway and anise. Of course, whenever I taste something amazing, I start thinking about how to turn it into ice cream, and so it hit me: Aquavit? What about Aquabeet! After all, the flavors of those spices go so well with root vegetables, and beets are a favorite in the Scandinavian countries where the spirit was born. So I made a simple syrup with grated beets, extracting their vivid purple color and earthy sweetness. Rather than skip the booze and stick with the spices, I decided to add aquavit to the syrup too, cooking off some of the alcohol so you get its clean grain flavor but not its burn.

1 cup Krogstad aquavit or one with a similar caraway-anise flavor profile

¼ teaspoon kosher salt

1 cup coarsely shredded peeled red beets

2 cups Sorbet Base (page 36), very cold

In a small pot, bring the aquavit, salt, and 1½ cups water to a boil and boil for 3 minutes. Turn off the heat, add the beets, cover, and let them steep until the mixture has cooled to room temperature.

Set a fine-mesh strainer over a heatproof bowl. Strain the mixture into the bowl, gently pressing on the beets to extract as much liquid as you can. Discard the beets. Let the mixture cool to room temperature, then chill until cold. You can use the cold syrup right away or store it in an airtight container in the fridge for up to 2 weeks.

Put the beet syrup and the sorbet base into a bowl and use a stick blender to briefly blend to combine. Pour the mixture into an ice cream maker and turn on the machine. Churn just until the mixture has the texture of a pourable frozen smoothie (see pages 23 to 24 for timing ranges, depending on the machine).

Transfer the sorbet, scraping every last delicious drop from the machine, into freezer-friendly containers. Cover with parchment paper, pressing it to the surface of the sorbet so it adheres, then cover with a lid. It's okay if the parchment hangs over the rim. Store it in the coldest part of your freezer (farthest from the door) until firm, at least 6 hours. It will keep for up to 3 months.

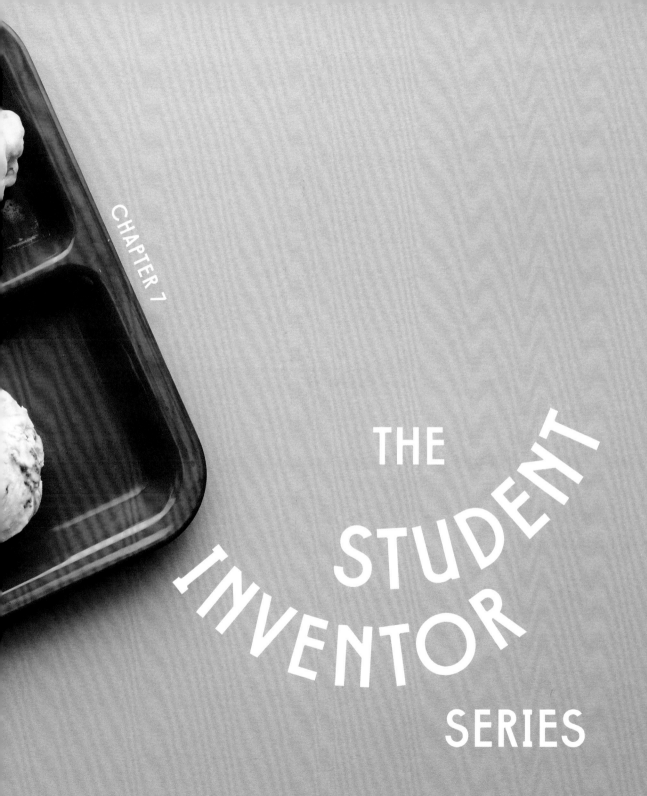

CHAPTER 7

THE
STUDENT
INVENTOR
SERIES

Every September, we present what is probably my favorite theme menu: our Student Inventor series. The ideas start with a challenge for the students of local schools: Imagine an ice cream flavor you've never seen before. And just like that, we mobilize an army of the most creative thinkers in the country.

Thousands of ideas pour in from kids who spend hours brainstorming the wildest combinations, sketching out the flavors to communicate the incommunicable. Our kitchen team sits down with heaps of submissions, cracking up as we call out our favorites—truly epic flavors that transcend simple deliciousness. We want ones whose names and accompanying drawings will give customers the same giggles and thrills they gave us.

After we've whittled down the submissions to a dozen or so—Lotsa Nacho, say, or Rainbow Unicorn Galaxy Swirl—comes the hard part: actually *making* the flavors. They usually require more care than any I dream up myself, but each one is an opportunity to show a kid that his or her dreams can literally become reality, that with passion and hard work, imagination can be spun into a scoop. Our goal is ice cream that the inventor recognizes at first lick— *that's my flavor!* We taste, think, taste, and

think until we painfully choose just five to be immortalized at our stores.

Everyone wins with this series: The students are pumped. Their schools get the proceeds. Customers get to taste the fruits of their and our labor. But I have a selfish reason for loving this, too. After years of relentless learning and experimentation, I'm no longer an amateur ice cream creator. A little too much knowledge occasionally makes me a party-pooper. I often shoot down my own ideas before they make it off the ground. Kids, on the other hand, are open to everything. Kids don't always follow rules. They're like I was when all I had was my $4 ice cream makers and a dream.

Okay, I do still have at least a little kid in me, since sometimes the students submit flavors that are already in the Salt & Straw pipeline. Either that, or I'd better watch out—the next generation of ice cream makers already has my number.

OLDE PEOPLE

MAKES ABOUT

2

PINTS

This head-turning flavor, perhaps the most unlikely in a roster full of unlikely flavors, was submitted by Charlotte, a student at Abernethy Elementary in southeast Portland. The name, complete with the old-timey "e," came with an imagined litany of grandfatherly tastes, the wisdom and trials and pleasures of age summed up by a combination of wheat germ and iced tea, Werther's candies and Bengay. Well, it turns out that between the slightly malty, tannic qualities of tea, the brightness of lemon, and the crunch and sweetness of Florentine cookies made from crushed Werther's candies and wheat germ, the combination actually tastes great! For the sake of deliciousness, we omitted the Bengay.

3 cups Ice Cream
Base (page 34),
very cold

1 tablespoon finely
grated lemon zest
(use a Microplane)

1 teaspoon Nestea
iced tea powder

1/8 teaspoon kosher
salt

3/4 cup broken
Werther's Wheat
Germ Florentines
(recipe follows)

Put the ice cream base, lemon zest, Nestea powder, and salt into a bowl and whisk to combine. Pour the mixture into an ice cream maker and turn on the machine. Churn just until the mixture has the texture of soft-serve (see pages 23 to 24 for timing ranges, depending on the machine).

Quickly transfer the ice cream into freezer-friendly containers: Spoon in a layer of ice cream, sprinkle on some florentine pieces, and use a spoon to press them in gently. Repeat. Cover with parchment paper, pressing it to the surface of the ice cream so it adheres, then cover with a lid. It's okay if the parchment hangs over the rim. Store it in the coldest part of your freezer (farthest from the door) until firm, at least 6 hours. It will keep for up to 3 months.

WERTHER'S WHEAT GERM FLORENTINES

MAKES ABOUT 1 CUP OF COOKIE PIECES

10 pieces Werther's Original caramel hard candies

1 tablespoon heavy cream

3 tablespoons unsalted butter

$\frac{1}{4}$ cup granulated sugar

$\frac{1}{4}$ cup wheat germ

2 tablespoons all-purpose flour

$\frac{1}{4}$ teaspoon vanilla extract

$\frac{1}{4}$ teaspoon kosher salt

Heat the oven to 300°F and line a sheet pan with parchment paper.

Using a rolling pin, food processor, or your tool of choice, crush the Werther's into small, pebbly pieces. In a small saucepan, combine $\frac{1}{2}$ cup water, the cream, and the crushed Werther's and cook over medium heat, stirring often, until the candy has liquefied, about 3 minutes. Raise the heat to medium-high and bring the mixture to a boil. Remove the pan from heat and stir in the butter and sugar, making sure the sugar is completely incorporated. Return the pan to medium heat, and bring it back to a boil. Boil until the mixture registers 235°F on a candy thermometer. Remove the pan from the heat and stir in the wheat germ, flour, vanilla, and salt.

Pour the mixture onto the lined sheet pan and use the back of a spoon or a spatula to spread it out in an even layer, as thin as you can (about $\frac{1}{16}$ inch). Bake in the oven until it turns golden brown, the edges begin to darken, and it's fully crisp, 8 to 10 minutes. Let the cookie cool to room temperature, then break it into 1-inch pieces. Store them in an airtight container at room temperature for up to 1 week.

THE KAIL CREEASHEON

MAKES ABOUT

2

PINTS

This creation of Elly, a first-grader at Portland's Abernethy Elementary, was as ingeniously conceived as her submission was creatively spelled: "This is enspired by my faveret kale saled! Vinily/wallnut ice creem with parmesan cheese and crushed short bread coocy toped with a kale chip." We toiled to incorporate the savory twists, not stopping until we had made an ice cream worthy of the term *cree-asheon*. Finally, we had it: kale brittle to mimic the crunch of the chip and Parmesan to up the umami of white chocolate fudge. Just like misspelled words, this flavor shouldn't make sense . . . but it does.

WHAT WE LEARN: *Without protection, most crunchy ingredients in ice cream will get soggy pretty quickly. That's where brittle comes in. The hard candy coating amplifies the crunch and provides a barrier that prevents moisture from soggying whatever you've encased inside—from pumpkin seeds to kale chips to crispy turkey skin.*

½ cup chopped walnuts

½ cup heavy cream

½ cup whole milk

¼ cup (lightly packed) light brown sugar

3 cups Ice Cream Base (page 34), very cold

1 teaspoon vanilla extract, preferably Mexican

½ teaspoon kosher salt

1 cup chopped Shortbread Cookies (recipe follows)

1 cup Kale Brittle pieces (recipe follows)

1 cup Parmesan Fudge Sauce (recipe follows)

In a medium pot set over medium heat, toast the walnuts, stirring them frequently, until they begin to get toasty and brown, 3 to 5 minutes. Add the cream, milk, and brown sugar and reduce the heat to medium-low. Cover the pot and cook, stirring the mixture occasionally, until it is thick and medium brown, 20 minutes. Remove the pot from the heat and pour the mixture through a fine-mesh strainer into a container. Chill the walnut cream in the fridge until cold, then strain out the spent walnuts. Use immediately or refrigerate for up to 2 days.

Put the ice cream base, walnut cream, vanilla, and salt into a bowl and whisk to combine. Pour the mixture into an ice cream maker and turn on the machine. Churn just until the mixture has the texture of soft-serve (see pages 23 to 24 for timing ranges, depending on the machine).

Transfer the ice cream mixture into freezer-friendly containers, sprinkling in some shortbread and kale brittle and drizzling thin ribbons of the Parmesan fudge in a spiral after each spoonful.

Cover with parchment paper, pressing it to the surface of the ice cream so it adheres, then cover with a lid. It's okay if the parchment hangs over the rim. Store it in the coldest part of your freezer (farthest from the door) until firm, at least 6 hours. It will keep for up to 3 months.

SHORTBREAD COOKIES

MAKES ABOUT 2 CUPS OF CHOPPED COOKIES

8 tablespoons (1 stick) cold unsalted butter, cut into chunks

1/3 cup granulated sugar

3/4 cup all-purpose flour

1/4 cup cornstarch

1/2 teaspoon vanilla extract

1/2 teaspoon kosher salt

Heat the oven to 325°F. Line a sheet pan with parchment paper.

In a stand mixer fitted with the paddle attachment, cream the butter and sugar, mixing on medium-high speed until the butter takes on a lighter color, about 2 minutes. Stop the mixer and add the flour, cornstarch, vanilla, and salt. Return the mixer to medium-low speed and stir until the mixture is just combined and slightly pebbly.

Dump the dough onto the lined sheet pan, press it together, and use a rolling pin to roll it to about a ¼-inch thickness. Bake until the shortbread is golden brown around the edges, about 25 minutes.

Let the shortbread cool to room temperature. Then cut the cookie into small pieces (¼- to ½-inch) and use them immediately or store them in the freezer until ready to use.

PARMESAN FUDGE SAUCE

MAKES ABOUT 1 CUP

1 cup white chocolate chips

1/8 teaspoon xanthan gum (Yes, I'm easy to find! See page 33.)

4 ounces Parmesan cheese, sliced

1/2 cup light corn syrup

1/4 cup heavy cream

1/2 teaspoon kosher salt

In a medium mixing bowl, combine the white chocolate chips and xanthan gum.

In a small saucepan, combine the Parmesan, ½ cup water, corn syrup, cream, and salt. Cook over low heat, stirring occasionally, until the cheese is partially melted and slightly gooey, 10 minutes. Use a fine-mesh strainer set over a bowl to strain out any remaining solid cheese. Yes, you can eat the cheese, but first, immediately pour the strained hot cheese over the white chocolate chips.

Let the mixture sit for about 2 minutes, until the chocolate melts. Then pour the mixture into a blender and blend until smooth. Let it cool to just above room temperature (so it's still liquid) before using. It will keep in the fridge for up to 1 week; warm it gently before using, just to re-melt it.

KALE BRITTLE

MAKES ABOUT 3 CUPS OF CRUSHED CANDY

3 dinosaur (a.k.a.
Tuscan or lacinato)
kale leaves,
rinsed and dried

1 teaspoon vegetable
oil

½ teaspoon kosher
salt, plus a pinch

1 cup granulated
sugar

⅓ cup light corn
syrup

8 tablespoons
(1 stick) unsalted
butter, cut into
1-inch pieces

1 teaspoon baking
soda

Heat the oven to 300°F.

Tear the kale leaves from the stems, keeping the leaves in very large pieces. Discard the stems. Put the leaves on a sheet pan and drizzle the vegetable oil over them. Sprinkle with the pinch of salt, and use your hands to rub the oil into all the crevices of the kale. Spread the kale in a single layer on the sheet pan and bake until the leaves are perfectly crisp but not dark nor burnt, 10 to 15 minutes.

Let the kale cool to room temperature, then break it up into ¼-inch pieces.

Line a sheet pan with parchment paper.

Combine the sugar, corn syrup, and ¼ cup water in a medium saucepan, and stir until all of the sugar looks wet. Set the pan over medium-high heat and cook, stirring occasionally, until the sugar has completely melted, about 3 minutes.

Continue to cook, this time covered and without stirring, until the mixture has thickened slightly, about 3 minutes. Add the butter and the ½ teaspoon salt, then immediately stir until the butter has completely melted. Attach a candy thermometer to the side of the pan. Let the mixture simmer away until it registers 300°F on the thermometer.

Remove the pan from the heat, and quickly but thoroughly stir in the kale chips, doing your best to distribute the chips throughout the sticky mixture. Quickly and thoroughly stir in the baking soda (watch it all bubble!). Immediately pour the mixture onto the lined sheet pan, then quickly use a butter knife or a metal spatula to spread it out into a relatively even layer that's just under ¼ inch thick. Let the brittle sit uncovered until it has cooled to room temperature, about 1 hour.

Use your hands to break the brittle into irregular bite-size pieces. Use now or store them in an airtight container in the freezer until ready to use as a mix-in (or to simply eat), up to 3 months. There's no need to defrost before using.

CHOCOLATE SARDINES

While this suggests avant-garde ice cream at its most perplexing, this flavor is just the opposite. Instead of high-end culinary creativity, we're talking about cozy milk chocolate ice cream classed up with an elegant tartare of fish—of the Swedish gummy variety. For this ode to the pleasures of chocolate-coated chewies, we fashion a sort of Swedish Fish Jell-O to skirt the candy-gets-hard-in-the-freezer problem and keep the tartare good and chewy.

¼ cup granulated sugar

¼ cup unsweetened cocoa powder (any kind, but Dutch-processed is especially great here)

3 cups Ice Cream Base (page 34), very cold

1 cup Swedish Fish Tartare (recipe follows)

Combine the sugar and ¼ cup water in a small saucepan, set it over medium heat, and bring to a boil. Remove the pan from the heat and whisk in the cocoa powder until the mixture is smooth and glossy. Transfer it to an airtight container and let it cool to room temperature. If using a frozen-bowl type of machine, chill the mixture until cold.

Put the cocoa mixture and the ice cream base into a bowl and whisk to combine. Pour the mixture into an ice cream maker and turn on the machine. Churn just until the mixture has the texture of soft-serve (see pages 23 to 24 for timing ranges, depending on the machine).

Quickly transfer the ice cream into freezer-friendly containers: Spoon in a layer of ice cream, sprinkle on some fish tartare, and use a spoon to press it in gently. Repeat. Cover with parchment paper, pressing it to the surface of the ice cream so it adheres, then cover with a lid. It's okay if the parchment hangs over the rim. Store it in the coldest part of your freezer (farthest from the door) until firm, at least 6 hours. It will keep for up to 3 months.

SWEDISH FISH TARTARE

MAKES ABOUT 2 CUPS OF DICED GUMMY PIECES

5 ounces Swedish
Fish candies

1 tablespoon
unflavored powdered
gelatin

Prepare a 9-inch square sheet pan or airtight container by lightly spraying it with nonstick cooking spray.

In a small saucepan, combine the Swedish Fish and 1½ cups water and bring the water to a gentle simmer over medium-low heat. Simmer, stirring occasionally, until the fish are a little more than halfway melted into a clear red syrup, about 10 minutes.

Meanwhile, in a small bowl, combine the powdered gelatin and 2 tablespoons cold water, stirring lightly with a spoon to mix well. Let the gelatin sit in the water for about 1 minute.

When the fish syrup is ready, remove the pan from the heat and add the gelatin, stirring gently until well combined.

Pour the fish syrup through a fine-mesh strainer into the prepared container, discarding the solids. Cover it tightly, and chill it overnight in the freezer.

Pop the frozen fish jelly out of the container by turning it over and wiggling it out. Cut the jelly into ¼-inch cubes if you are using it right away, or store it uncut in an airtight container in the freezer for up to 1 month.

SKITTLES RAINBOW SHERBET

MAKES
5
PINTS

For our ice creams, we source chocolate from the most decorated artisans, we look for beer from the most talented brewers, and we buy the wildest wild berries from the most dedicated foragers. We will seek good ingredients wherever they may be, even if that's in the supermarket checkout line. We got this particular lead from local candy-aisle maven Addie, who suggested employing the chewy nubs of joy contained in those iconic red Skittles bags. To give them their due, we got to thinking of a kaleidoscopic scoop, a special flavor that requires some patience as well as an ice cream maker capable of churning multiple batches without rest. The fuss is worth it, though, to truly *experience*, not just taste, the rainbow.

WHAT WE LEARN: *Here we separately churn several sherbets of different colors and flavors, layer them sideways in containers as they finish, and freeze it all to make a rainbow scoop. Yet there's no reason to limit yourself to one type of frozen treat. Try pairing rich ice cream with bright sorbets in the same container, which gives you a contrast in textures and allows you to manipulate the eating experience, since you'll taste the flavor of the sorbet first and that of the ice cream last.*

5 2.17-ounce bags of Skittles

2½ cups Sorbet Base (page 36), very cold

1⅔ cups heavy cream

1⅔ cups whole milk

½ cup plus 2 tablespoons freshly squeezed lemon juice

Kosher salt

First separate out all of the Skittles into red, orange, yellow, green, and purple and put the candies of each color in individual small bowls.

Now, this part is easy but sounds complicated. Add ½ cup water to one of the bowls of Skittles and pour the mixture into a small pot. Cook over medium heat, stirring occasionally, until most of the Skittles have melted into the water, about 3 minutes. Pour the liquid through a fine-mesh strainer into its own small bowl, straining out any bits of Skittle that refused to melt. Repeat with the other colors, cleaning the pot and the strainer after each flavor, until all five are syrup-ified and in their separate bowls. Chill the syrups until they're cold to the touch before using.

Start with churning red: Put ½ cup of the sorbet base, ⅓ cup of the cream, ⅓ cup of the milk, 2 tablespoons of the lemon juice, a pinch of salt, and the red Skittle syrup into a bowl and whisk to combine. Pour the mixture into an ice cream maker and turn on the machine. Churn just until the mixture has the texture of a pourable frozen smoothie; because there is such a small amount, this should take a small fraction of the time it normally takes you to churn, as little as a few minutes, depending on your machine.

(recipe continues)

Transfer the sherbet, scraping every last delicious drop from the machine, into freezer-friendly containers, filling up only one-fifth of each container on the far left side. Cover each partially filled container and freeze them, laying them on their sides, until you're ready with the next color.

Repeat these churning and filling steps for the remaining colors, transferring the sherbet to each container in the order of the rainbow (red, orange, yellow, green, purple), cleaning your machine after each color and keeping the colors separated. The goal is for the final product to have five even rows of the different Skittles colors when the container is turned right-side up. (When you run a scoop over the surface, you'll get a rainbow scoop.)

Once you have finished with the last color, cover the rainbow sherbet with parchment paper, pressing it to the surface of the sherbet so it adheres, then cover with a lid. It's okay if the parchment hangs over the rim. Store it in the coldest part of your freezer (farthest from the door) until firm, at least 6 hours. It will keep for up to 3 months.

STOP, GUAC & ROLL

MAKES ABOUT

2

PINTS

An epic name for kindergartener Keziah's epic ice cream. This young culinary mastermind from Chapman Elementary, in Portland, envisioned not only a killer name but an extraordinarily delicious flavor made with avocado, tortillas, and cinnamon. The avocado makes a rich, buttery ice cream and the tortillas, fried and dusted churro-style with cinnamon and sugar, provide crunchy delight.

1 medium-size ripe avocado, pitted, peeled, and cut into chunks

³/₄ cup ice-cold water

¹/₄ cup heavy cream

¹/₃ cup whole milk

2 tablespoons freshly squeezed lime juice

2 cups Sorbet Base (page 36), very cold

³/₄ cup crushed Cinnamon Tortilla Crunch (recipe follows)

The following mixture will not keep, so make it when you are ready to churn the ice cream.

Put the avocado, ice-cold water, cream, milk, and lime juice in a blender or food processor and blend until the mixture is a velvety puree. Add the sorbet base and briefly blend to combine well.

Immediately pour the mixture into an ice cream maker and turn on the machine. Churn just until the mixture has the texture of soft-serve (see pages 23 to 24 for timing ranges, depending on the machine).

Quickly transfer the ice cream into freezer-friendly containers: Spoon in a layer of ice cream, sprinkle on some cinnamon tortilla crunch, and use a spoon to press it in gently. Repeat. Cover with parchment paper, pressing it to the surface of the ice cream so it adheres, then cover with a lid. It's okay if the parchment hangs over the rim. Store it in the coldest part of your freezer (farthest from the door) until firm, at least 6 hours. It will keep for up to 3 months.

CINNAMON TORTILLA CRUNCH

MAKES ABOUT 1 CUP OF CRUMBLED CHIPS

1 cup lightly crushed Juanita's corn tortilla chips (or your favorite brand)

4 tablespoons (½ stick) unsalted butter, melted

¼ cup granulated sugar

½ teaspoon ground cinnamon

⅛ teaspoon kosher salt

Heat the oven to 300°F.

Toss the chips, melted butter, sugar, cinnamon, and salt together in a bowl until the chips are evenly coated in sugar. Spread the chips in an even layer on a sheet pan and bake for 20 minutes, until golden brown.

Let the chips cool to room temperature, then store them, covered, at room temperature for up to 1 week. Crush the chips into small pieces before mixing them into the ice cream.

CHAPTER 8

THE
SPOOKTACULAR
SERIES

After the summer and early fall harvests of fruits and veggies, we usually take a break from getting creative with berries and cauliflower. We ease off collaborating with talented local distillers, jam makers, and other artisans around town. Instead, we join forces with the Crypt Keeper. In other words, boys and ghouls, we let our imaginations stumble into foggy graveyards, tiptoe up dark, creaky staircases, and peek under the bed.

The flavors we devise are meant to conjure up a particularly eerie time of year. I'm talking about an ice cream made with bugs, another made with real blood, a witch's brew that contains everything *but* eye of newt, and a spine-chilling take on biting into a ghost. In October, all of our shops offer the same spooky menu, because while some of the best food is local, fear is universal.

MAKES ABOUT
2
PINTS

Befitting a brew conjured by a coven, this sweet, mysterious concoction contains a virtual scavenger-hunt's worth of ingredients. Worry not, there's no Shakespearean eye of newt or toe of frog. The potion, known as "amortentia" and inspired by another great writer, J. K. Rowling, requires various tasty tonics thought to arouse vigor (ginseng royal jelly) and ardor (horny goat weed tea). But not even Hogwarts professor Horace Eugene Flaccus Slughorn would expect that throughout each ruby-red scoop, Pop Rocks lurk, coated with aphrodisiacs like rose and chocolate so that the little explosions they provide truly imitate the exhilaration of love.

¼ cup granulated sugar

1 tea bag pure ginkgo biloba tea

1 tea bag horny goat weed tea

2 tablespoons grated peeled red beets (use a Microplane)

2 cups Sorbet Base (page 36), very cold

In a small pot, bring 2½ cups water to a boil, whisk in the sugar, then reduce the heat so it just barely bubbles. Add the ginkgo biloba tea bag, the goat weed tea bag, and the grated beets and gently simmer for 8 minutes until the mixture is the color of red Kool-Aid and the teas have released their magical, love-inducing properties. Remove the pot from the heat and strain the mixture through a fine-mesh strainer into a large bowl and let it cool. Add the sorbet base, blood orange juice, royal jelly, citric acid, vanilla, salt, and cinnamon. Use a stick blender to briefly blend to combine well. Then chill until cold and use, or refrigerate for up to 3 days.

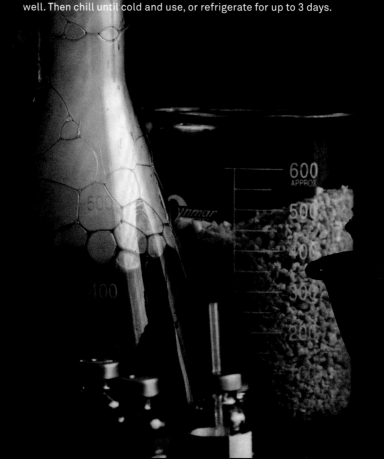

squeezed blood
orange juice

1 tablespoon ginseng
royal jelly

1½ teaspoons citric
acid or ¼ cup
freshly squeezed
lemon juice

¼ teaspoon vanilla
extract

⅛ teaspoon kosher
salt

⅛ teaspoon ground
cinnamon

½ cup White
Chocolate Rose
Pop Rocks pieces
(recipe follows)

¼ cup freeze-dried
strawberries (in
pea-size pieces)

Pour the sorbet into an ice cream maker and turn on the machine. Churn just until the mixture has the texture of a pourable frozen smoothie (see pages 23 to 24 for timing ranges, depending on the machine).

Quickly transfer the ice cream into freezer-friendly containers: Spoon in a layer of ice cream, sprinkle on some pop rocks and crumbled strawberries, and use a spoon to press them in gently. Repeat. Cover with parchment paper, pressing it to the surface of the sorbet so it adheres, then cover with a lid. It's okay if the parchment hangs over the rim. Store it in the coldest part of your freezer (farthest from the door) until firm, at least 6 hours. It will keep for up to 3 months.

WHITE CHOCOLATE ROSE POP ROCKS

MAKES ABOUT 2 CUPS OF POP ROCKS PIECES

$1/4$ cup white
chocolate chips

1 tablespoon
vegetable oil

6 drops Rose
Absolute Chef's
Essence (from
aftelier.com) or
food-grade rose
essential oil

$3/4$ cup unflavored
Pop Rocks (or
carbonated candy
known as "culinary
crystals")

Prepare a sheet pan by lining it with parchment paper.

If you are using a microwave, combine the white chocolate and vegetable oil in a microwave-safe bowl and microwave on low power, stirring the mixture occasionally, until it is fully melted. Or to use a double boiler, pour an inch or so of water into a small saucepan and bring it to a simmer. Combine the white chocolate and vegetable oil in a heatproof bowl that will sit on the saucepan without touching the water. Set the bowl on the pan and heat, stirring, until all of the chocolate is melted. Immediately remove the bowl from the heat.

Using a spatula, stir the chocolate with slow, methodical, wide, dramatic stirs so that you fold in as much cool air as possible and in the process cool the chocolate down until it's just warmer than body temperature. Gently stir in the rose oil.

Fold the Pop Rocks into the chocolate and stir *incredibly* gently until the Pop Rocks are completely coated. Pour the mixture onto the parchment-lined sheet pan and use the spatula to spread it out as thin as possible, being super gentle to prevent the rocks from popping.

Cool in the fridge until the chocolate is completely hardened, about 10 minutes. Then carefully (again to avoid popping the pop out of the Pop Rocks!) break the chocolate into ¼-inch pieces and use them immediately or store them in an airtight container in the fridge for up to 3 months.

ESSENCE OF GHOST

MAKES ABOUT
2
PINTS

You're walking alone down a dark hallway, the floorboards creaking beneath your wary steps. The only light comes from a single candle. As you walk past, it flickers out. You feel a frigid hand on your shoulder and you spin around to find . . . nothing. Then out of the corner of your eye you see a faint swirl of white. With as much excitement as fear, you spin around, reach out, and snatch a thick cloud of the ghost, then greedily shove it in your mouth. At last, you have the answer to a question you've never had the courage to ask: What do ghosts taste like? This bone-white sherbet holds the delicious answer, with a sweetness that vanishes as quickly as it appears, giving way to smoky, pleasantly bitter wisps of mysterious flavors that keep you wondering what you've just tasted.

2 cups Sorbet Base (page 36), very cold

3/4 cup heavy cream

1/2 cup whole milk

1/2 cup ice-cold water

1 tablespoon the peatiest scotch you can find, such as Laphroaig or Ardbeg

1/4 teaspoon kosher salt

1/8 teaspoon vanilla extract, preferably Mexican

3/4 cup Ghostly Ice Cream Wisps (recipe follows; see Note), tempered to a soft-serve consistency

Combine the sorbet base, cream, milk, ice-cold water, scotch, salt, and vanilla in a bowl and use a stick blender to briefly blend to combine well. Pour the mixture into an ice cream maker and turn it on. Churn just until the mixture has the texture of a pourable frozen smoothie (see pages 23 to 24 for timing ranges, depending on the machine).

Alternate spooning layers of the mixture and dollops of the ghostly ice cream wisps in freezer-friendly containers. After you finish packing each container, use a knife or chopstick to very gently swirl the contents together to ensure that the wisps are extra-wispy (the way you'd make a marbled cheesecake).

Cover with parchment paper, pressing it to the surface so it adheres, then cover with a lid. It's okay if the parchment hangs over the rim. Store it in the coldest part of your freezer (farthest from the door) until firm, at least 6 hours. It will keep for up to 3 months.

GHOSTLY ICE CREAM WISPS

MAKES ABOUT ¾ CUP

2 teaspoons black
   cocoa powder (see
   Note)

¾ cup Ice Cream
   Base (page 34),
   very cold

⅛ teaspoon kosher
   salt

⅛ teaspoon
   vanilla extract,
   preferably Mexican

⅛ teaspoon black
   food coloring
   (optional)

Put the cocoa powder in a small heatproof bowl and pour 2 teaspoons of boiling water over it. Use a fork to mix the mixture to make a smooth paste. Chill until cold.

Add the ice cream base, salt, vanilla, and food coloring, if using, to the chilled cocoa paste, stir well, then pour the mixture into an ice cream maker. Turn on the machine and churn until the mixture reaches the texture of a milkshake (slightly looser than what we typically look for; since this is such a small quantity, it may take only a few minutes).

Transfer the ice cream to an airtight container and store it in the coldest part of your freezer (farthest from the door) until firm, at least 6 hours. It will keep for up to 3 months. Before scooping it, let the frozen ice cream sit at room temperature until it is the texture of soft-serve.

NOTE

To make this flavor all at once, you'll need an extra freezer bowl or ice cream maker with a compressor to handle more than one batch in a row. Otherwise, you'll have to make the Ghostly Ice Cream Wisps first, then refreeze your machine's bowl for 24 hours to make the base of the ice cream.

Best known for giving Oreos their dark color and pleasantly bitter quality, black cocoa is a variety of Dutch-processed powder that is extra alkalized. Look for it at specialty grocery stores, stores devoted to baking, and online.

CREEPY CRAWLY CRITTERS

MAKES ABOUT
2
PINTS

Here's an ice cream that starts off bright and cheery, like your mood on a sunny fall day. Flavored with vivid green matcha to evoke a grassy field, and orange and tequila to conjure up the tipsy sensation provided by a slight chill in the air and colorful leaves in the trees, this ice cream soon turns eerily delicious as you discover the surprise in each scoop: a veritable swarm of grasshoppers, ants, and other insects, trapped in chocolate and hard-candy amber by the entomological geniuses at Don Bugito (donbugito.com) in Oakland, California. It's as if you were running through that field of grass, then tripped face-first into a patch of teeming, squirming bugs. Yet don't be afraid—they're tasty, nutritious, and slightly malty.

1 tablespoon reposado tequila

1 tablespoon freshly squeezed orange juice

2 teaspoons matcha powder

3 cups Ice Cream Base (page 34), very cold

One 1.5-ounce bag Don Bugito Coconut Toffee-Brittle Bugitos

Two 0.8-ounce bags Don Bugito Dark Chocolate Covered Crickets

In a large bowl, combine the tequila, orange juice, and matcha and whisk until most of the clumps are out. Whisk in the ice cream base. Then pass the mixture through a fine-mesh strainer into a bowl to ensure there aren't any remaining clumps of matcha. Pour it into an ice cream maker and turn on the machine. Churn just until the mixture has the texture of soft-serve (see pages 23 to 24 for timing ranges, depending on the machine).

Quickly transfer the ice cream into freezer-friendly containers: Spoon in a layer of ice cream, sprinkle on some bugitos and crickets, and use a spoon to press them in gently. Repeat. Cover with parchment paper, pressing it to the surface of the ice cream so it adheres, then cover with a lid. It's okay if the parchment hangs over the rim. Store it in the coldest part of your freezer (farthest from the door) until firm, at least 6 hours. It will keep for up to 1 month (much longer and the brittle starts to dissolve).

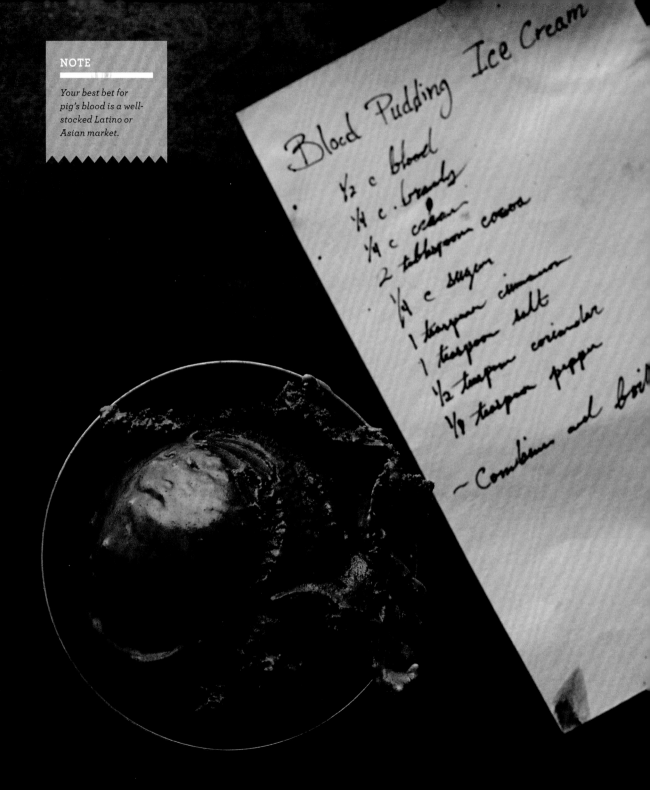

Blood Pudding Ice Cream

• ½ c blood
• ¼ c. brandy
• ¼ c cream
2 tablespoon cocoa
½ c sugar
1 teaspoon cinnamon
1 teaspoon salt
½ teaspoon coriander
½ teaspoon pepper

— Combine and boil

GRANDMA DRACULA'S BLOOD PUDDING

MAKES ABOUT
2
PINTS

If vampires passed recipes down from generation to generation, then little blood-suckers everywhere would be deciphering Grandma Dracula's Romanian chicken scratch and churning blood into ice cream gold. Fear not, we've carefully toed the line between delectable and frightful. The flavor is a heady mix of spices, cocoa, and cream cooked into real blood pudding and spun into a treat that will make you squirm—with delight.

1 cup heavy cream

½ cup pig's blood (thawed, if frozen; see Note)

¼ cup brandy

⅓ cup granulated sugar

2 tablespoons unsweetened cocoa powder, preferably Guittard's Cocoa Rouge

One 2-inch cinnamon stick

1 teaspoon kosher salt

½ teaspoon coriander seeds

¼ teaspoon black peppercorns

3 cups Ice Cream Base (page 34), very cold

In a small saucepan, combine the cream, blood, brandy, sugar, cocoa powder, cinnamon stick, salt, coriander seeds, and peppercorns and thoroughly whisk the ingredients together. Then set the pan over medium-low heat and cook, stirring constantly, until the blood mixture thickens (enough to coat the back of a spoon), about 8 minutes. Toward the end, use an instant-read thermometer to ensure that the mixture registers 160°F. Remove the pan from the heat and let the mixture sit for 10 to 15 minutes to cool slightly and steep the spices. Then pour it through a fine-mesh strainer into a container and discard the peppercorns, coriander seeds, and cinnamon stick. Chill until cold and the mixture has a pudding-like consistency, about 3 hours. Use right away or store in the fridge in an airtight container with a layer of plastic wrap directly on the surface for up to 2 days.

Put the ice cream base and the blood pudding into a bowl and use a stick blender to briefly blend to combine well. Pour the mixture into an ice cream maker and turn on the machine. Churn just until the mixture has the texture of soft-serve (see pages 23 to 24 for timing ranges, depending on the machine).

Transfer the ice cream, scraping every last delicious drop from the machine, into freezer-friendly containers. Cover with parchment paper, pressing it to the surface of the ice cream so it adheres, then cover with a lid. It's okay if the parchment hangs over the rim. Store it in the coldest part of your freezer (farthest from the door) until firm, at least 6 hours. It will keep for up to 3 months.

MAKES ABOUT
2½
PINTS

For this one, we channeled our inner child and metaphorically emptied our candy bags into ice cream. Yet unlike the Halloweens of our youth, instead of going door to door, we decided that we'd go pot to pot, making our favorite treats—Snickers, Whoppers, Heath Bars, and Reese's Peanut Butter Cups—ourselves. It takes us 23 days to do it at Salt & Straw, but at home, it'll take a bit less time to raid the store for your top picks, then pack them so generously into salty butterscotch ice cream that it'll make both Ben and Jerry cringe.

- ¼ cup (lightly packed) light brown sugar
- 1 tablespoon granulated sugar
- 1 tablespoon light corn syrup
- 2 tablespoons bourbon
- ¼ cup heavy cream
- 1 teaspoon unsalted butter
- ⅛ teaspoon vanilla extract
- ⅛ teaspoon kosher salt

In a small saucepan, combine the brown sugar, granulated sugar, corn syrup, and bourbon. Stir until all of the sugar looks wet. Put the pan over medium heat and cook until the sugar is completely melted and is beginning to boil, 2 to 3 minutes. Continue to cook, without stirring just until the sugar begins to smoke a bit (you do want a little bit of burn!), another 5 to 7 minutes. Remove the pan from the heat and immediately add the cream to stop the burning. Stir until everything is completely melted together into butterscotch sauce. Stir in the butter, vanilla, and salt and cool to room temperature before using. (You can store it, refrigerated, for up to 1 week, but let it come to room temperature before using.)

Base (page 34), very cold

¾ cup frozen chopped Snickers (from 2 regular bars)

¾ cup frozen chopped Reese's Peanut Butter Cups (from 6 peanut butter cups)

½ cup frozen chopped Heath Bars (from 2 regular bars)

½ cup frozen chopped Whoppers (from one 1.75-ounce bag)

Put the ice cream base and the butterscotch sauce into a bowl and whisk to combine. If you're using a frozen-bowl type of machine, cover and chill in the fridge until cold. Pour the mixture into an ice cream maker and turn on the machine. Churn just until the mixture has the texture of soft-serve (see pages 23 to 24 for timing ranges, depending on the machine).

Quickly transfer the ice cream, scraping every last delicious drop from the machine, into a mixing bowl. Quickly and gently fold the Snickers, Reese's, Heath Bars, and Whoppers into the ice cream so they're well distributed. Transfer to freezer-friendly containers and cover with parchment paper, pressing it to the surface of the ice cream so it adheres, then cover with a lid. It's okay if the parchment hangs over the rim. Store it in the coldest part of your freezer (farthest from the door) until firm, at least 6 hours. It will keep for up to 3 months.

CHAPTER 9

THE

THANKSGIVING

TABLE-TO-CONE

SERIES

Like the holiday it celebrates, this collection is meant to bring people together. And like the holiday it celebrates, it should make them argue a little, too.

Don't worry, they won't be arguing about religion or politics—these are fun spats, provoked by scoops that harness Thanksgiving flavors and then turn them upside down. They're particularly fun to eat at the table, friends and family passing around all five pints and oohing, aahing, and sometimes gasping. In fact, they make the most sense when enjoyed all together. Alone, turkey ice cream seems pretty weird.

Okay, it *is* a little weird, though the polarizing flavor has converted countless skeptics with its crunchy turkey-crackling brittle and the way its mild, meaty yumminess plays well with sugar—as anyone who has ever slathered a leftovers sandwich with sweet potatoes can attest. Mashed potatoes and gravy (spiked with white chocolate) and cranberry-apple stuffing (stuffing is basically bread pudding) also win over doubters with their tightrope walks between sweet and savory. Safer but no less exhilarating are pumpkin pie custard with tangy goat cheese to offset the sugar, and sweet potato casserole, which, let's face it, is essentially a dessert that we serve for dinner.

Don't worry, though, even we drew the line at green bean casserole.

SWEET POTATO CASSEROLE
WITH MAPLE PECANS

MAKES ABOUT
2½
PINTS

Each November we offer this full-bodied, cinnamon-scented sweet potato ice cream, as velvety as the Thanksgiving classic. To stay true to the version served at my family's table, we bring on the marshmallows, here as streaks of light-as-air fluff sweetened with dark maple syrup. Praline-ified pecans provide welcome crunch and saltiness. At Salt & Straw, we cook the sweet potatoes forever to minimize their starchiness (and eliminate the risk of a gummy texture). At home, I'm a big fan of canned sweet potatoes, which are already cooked to heck!

One 15-ounce can sweet potatoes in light syrup

⅓ cup (lightly packed) light brown sugar

½ teaspoon kosher salt

1 teaspoon ground cinnamon

3 cups Ice Cream Base (page 34), very cold

½ cup Brown Sugar Pecan Praline (recipe follows)

¾ cup Maple Marshmallow Fluff (recipe follows)

Heat the oven to 350°F.

Pour the sweet potatoes, syrup and all, into a baking dish. Add the brown sugar, salt, and cinnamon and stir until thoroughly combined. Cover the dish and bake in the oven for 35 minutes or until the potatoes are super mushy. Coarsely mash them.

Transfer 1 cup of the mashed sweet potatoes to a heatproof measuring cup, reserving the rest for another time. (It'll keep in the freezer for up to 2 months. Thaw and gently warm before using.)

Let the 1 cup of sweet potato mixture cool until it's slightly warm. Then combine it and the ice cream base in a blender, and blend until smooth. Chill until the mixture is cold.

Pour the mixture into an ice cream maker and turn on the machine. Churn just until the mixture has the texture of soft-serve (see pages 23 to 24 for timing ranges, depending on the machine).

Quickly transfer the ice cream into freezer-friendly containers: Spoon in layers of ice cream, sprinkles of praline, using a spoon to press them in gently, and a few generous dollops of maple fluff. Repeat.

Cover with parchment paper, pressing it to the surface of the ice cream so it adheres, then cover with a lid. It's okay if the parchment hangs over the rim. Store it in the coldest part of your freezer (farthest from the door) until firm, at least 6 hours. It will keep for up to 3 months.

BROWN SUGAR PECAN PRALINE

MAKES ABOUT 1 CUP

½ cup whole milk

2 tablespoons granulated sugar

2 tablespoons (lightly packed) light brown sugar

1 tablespoon unsalted butter

⅛ teaspoon vanilla extract

½ cup chopped pecans

Line a sheet pan with parchment paper and coat the paper lightly with nonstick cooking spray.

In a medium saucepan, combine the milk, granulated sugar, brown sugar, butter, and vanilla, stir well, and attach a candy thermometer. Set the pan over medium heat and cook, stirring often, until the mixture registers 238°F on the thermometer. (It's okay if it starts to crystallize.) Immediately stir in the pecans so they're completely coated. Keep stirring until the sugar begins to crystallize and become crumbly, about 20 seconds more.

Remove the pan from the heat and let the mixture cool until it's as thick as warm caramel, 5 to 10 minutes. Stir again, then scrape the mixture onto the prepared sheet pan, spreading it out to get the pecans in a more or less single layer. Let the praline cool to room temperature.

Remove the praline from the sheet pan, peel off the parchment, and crumble the praline into approximately ¼-inch pieces. Freeze them until cold and then use in the ice cream or transfer to freezer bags and freeze for up to 2 months.

MAPLE MARSHMALLOW FLUFF

MAKES ABOUT 4 CUPS

3 large egg whites (without even a spot of yolk!)

½ teaspoon cream of tartar

½ cup granulated sugar

¼ cup light corn syrup

⅓ cup dark, robust maple syrup

In a stand mixer fitted with the whisk attachment, beat the egg whites on medium-high speed until they're foamy, about 2 minutes. Add the cream of tartar and continue to beat until the whites reach the soft peak stage, about 3 minutes. Reduce the mixer speed to the lowest setting and leave it on while you heat the sugar.

Mix the sugar, 2 tablespoons water, the corn syrup, and the maple syrup in a medium saucepan, and attach a candy thermometer. Set the pan over medium-high heat and cook, stirring constantly, until the syrup turns clear, about 2 minutes. Then keep cooking, without stirring, until the syrup registers 238°F on the thermometer. Immediately remove the pan from the heat.

Raise the mixer speed to medium-low and drizzle the hot sugar syrup into the egg whites in a thin, steady stream, aiming for the hot syrup to hit only the whites and not the bowl. Once all of the syrup is incorporated, raise the mixer speed to medium-high and whip the fluff until it is just warm to the touch and has a glossy sheen, about 2 minutes. It will keep in an airtight container in the fridge for up to 2 weeks.

BUTTERED MASHED POTATOES & GRAVY

MAKES ABOUT

MAKES ABOUT
2½
PINTS

I'm always up for the challenge of capturing the pleasures of a piping-hot classic in below-freezing form. Mashed potatoes were a natural choice—the sight of a creamy mountain erupting with hot gravy has always kind of reminded me of a scoop of vanilla dripping with hot fudge. The flavor here is sweet, but salty and buttery, too. Yet the fun isn't done! Ribbons of white chocolate gravy made with chicken stock (and even a dose of bouillon, to propel the savory flavor through all that cream and sugar) make each lick a mind-bending thrill that'll transport you back to your first meal at the adults' table.

WHAT WE LEARN: *This recipe succeeds because of Michael Voltaggio,* Top Chef *winner and L.A. chef, who figured out how to produce ice cream with a gelato-like density and just enough starch to resemble fluffy mashed potatoes. The key is intentionally over-boiling Yukon Golds—which zaps the starch of a lot of its thickening power so it doesn't make our ice cream as stiff as . . . potatoes. Then we incorporate them, with brown butter, egg yolk, and a little sour cream, into our ice cream base.*

2 tablespoons unsalted butter

½ cup light corn syrup

5 ounces Yukon Gold potato (1 small), peeled and cut into ½-inch dice

1 large egg yolk

1 tablespoon sour cream

1 teaspoon kosher salt

3 cups Ice Cream Base (page 34), very cold

¼ cup White Chocolate Gravy (recipe follows)

Melt the butter in a small saucepan set over medium heat and keep cooking until it turns a light golden color, about 3 minutes. Add ½ cup water, the corn syrup, and the diced potato, raise the heat to high, and cook, stirring occasionally, until the mixture begins to boil. Reduce the heat to a gentle simmer, cover the pan, and cook, stirring occasionally, until the potatoes are very tender, 20 to 25 minutes. Take the pan off the heat and let the mixture cool, uncovered, to about room temperature.

Add the egg yolk, sour cream, and salt to the potatoes in the saucepan, and immediately use a stick blender to blend or whisk to form a very smooth, sticky mashed potato puree. Let it cool slightly. Add the ice cream base, blend briefly to combine, and transfer it to an airtight container and keep in the fridge until fully chilled, at least 4 hours or up to 3 days.

Pour the mixture into an ice cream maker and turn the machine on. Churn just until the mixture has the texture of soft-serve (see pages 23 to 24 for timing ranges, depending on the machine).

Meanwhile, if necessary, very gently warm the white chocolate gravy so it's drizzle-able but not so warm that it'll melt the ice cream.

Alternate spooning layers of the ice cream and drizzling on a tiny layer of the gravy in a spiral in freezer-friendly containers.

Cover with parchment paper, pressing it to the surface of the ice cream so it adheres, then cover with a lid. It's okay if the parchment hangs over the rim. Store it in the coldest part of your freezer (farthest from the door) until firm, at least 6 hours. It will keep for up to 3 months.

WHITE CHOCOLATE GRAVY

MAKES ABOUT 1 CUP

$1/2$ cup light corn syrup

$1/4$ cup heavy cream

2 tablespoons chicken stock

1 chicken bouillon cube

$1/8$ teaspoon xanthan gum (Yes, I'm easy to find! See page 33.)

$1/8$ teaspoon unsweetened cocoa powder (natural or Dutch-processed)

$1/2$ cup white chocolate chips

$1/8$ teaspoon kosher salt

Combine the corn syrup, cream, chicken stock, and chicken bouillon cube in a medium saucepan. Set it over medium-high heat and cook, stirring occasionally, until it comes to a boil and the bouillon has dissolved, about 3 minutes. Remove from the heat.

While the mixture is hot, sprinkle in the xanthan gum and cocoa powder, and whisk vigorously (or insert a stick blender and blend) for about 30 seconds to get the cocoa mixed in well. Add the white chocolate chips and the salt, and let the mixture sit until the chocolate is mostly melted, about 2 minutes. Whisk or blend again until the chocolate is completely melted and looks like yummy, satiny gravy. Transfer the gravy to a heatproof container and let it cool to room temperature.

Use it right away or refrigerate it in an airtight container for up to 2 weeks.

CRANBERRY-APPLE STUFFING

MAKES ABOUT
2½
PINTS

Equal parts sweet and savory, this scoop showcases stuffing swirled into celery-soda ice cream. It's so good you might start serving it alongside your turkey! Before you crinkle your nose at stuffing in ice cream, keep in mind that the line between stuffing and bread pudding is a fine one. We make ours with custard-soaked Hawaiian bread and stud it with bright chunks of Granny Smiths and blobs of cranberry sauce. (The canned kind is perfect here because it stays jelly-like even after baking and freezing.) Celery, the unsung hero of stuffing if you ask me, comes in the form of Dr. Brown's Cel-Ray soda, which has improbably survived extinction over the past century and a half.

One 12-ounce can Dr. Brown's Cel-Ray soda

3 cups Ice Cream Base (page 34), very cold

1 cup Cranberry-Apple Stuffing Chunks (recipe follows)

Pour the soda into a small saucepan and bring it to a boil over high heat. Reduce the heat and simmer vigorously until it reduces to ½ cup (pour it into a heatproof measuring cup to check), 10 to 15 minutes. Let it cool to room temperature, then cover and chill in the fridge until cold or for up to 1 week.

Put the ice cream base and celery soda syrup into a bowl and whisk to combine. Pour the mixture into an ice cream maker and turn on the machine. Churn just until the mixture has the texture of soft-serve (see pages 23 to 24 for timing ranges, depending on the machine).

Quickly transfer the ice cream into freezer-friendly containers: Spoon in a layer of ice cream, sprinkle on some of the stuffing, and use a spoon to press it in gently. Repeat. Cover with parchment paper, pressing it to the surface of the ice cream so it adheres, then cover with a lid. It's okay if the parchment hangs over the rim. Store it in the coldest part of your freezer (farthest from the door) until firm, at least 6 hours. It will keep for up to 3 months.

CRANBERRY-APPLE STUFFING CHUNKS

MAKES ABOUT 3 CUPS

1 cup cubed (½-inch cubes) soft, sweet eggy bread, such as challah or Hawaiian bread

1 medium Granny Smith apple (or any tart, crisp baking apple)

2 tablespoons unsalted butter

¼ cup (lightly packed) light brown sugar

2 tablespoons dried cranberries

2 large whole eggs

2 large egg yolks

½ cup heavy cream

½ cup granulated sugar

½ teaspoon kosher salt

⅛ teaspoon freshly ground black pepper

¼ cup jellied cranberry sauce, preferably Ocean Spray

Heat the oven to 250°F.

Spread the bread cubes in a single layer in a baking dish and bake until they are completely dried all the way through but not yet browned, about 15 minutes.

Meanwhile, peel, core, and cut the apple into ¼-inch dice. Melt the butter in a large saucepan over medium heat. Stir in the apples, brown sugar, and dried cranberries, and cook, stirring occasionally, until the apples are tender but still slightly crisp, about 5 minutes.

In a large bowl, whisk the eggs and egg yolks together until they're homogenous. Whisk in the cream, sugar, salt, and black pepper, then fold in the dried bread cubes and the apple mixture so the bread is completely coated in the egg. Cover with plastic wrap pressed directly on the surface of the mixture and let it soak at room temperature for at least 15 or up to 30 minutes.

Heat the oven to 350°F.

Give the bread mixture one big stir, then transfer it to a standard-size loaf pan, pressing gently so it's in a nice even layer. Add the cranberry sauce, dropping teaspoon-size dollops evenly on top and nudging them so they're just below the surface of the bread mixture. Bake uncovered until the center is cooked through (a toothpick inserted into the middle should come out clean), 30 to 35 minutes.

Let the stuffing cool, then cut it into ¾-inch chunks and refrigerate in the baking dish for up to 1 week.

SALTED CARAMEL
THANKSGIVING TURKEY

MAKES ABOUT
2½
PINTS

You might be surprised to learn that when I first conceived of this mind-bending flavor, it didn't occur to me that it would strike people as weird. After all, we had already decided to translate the most pivotal Thanksgiving dishes into ice cream, so a turkey flavor didn't seem controversial so much as it did inevitable. We slowly cook flavorful turkey skin until it's super crunchy, then use that lovely rendered fat to replace butter in a classic caramel (or *sorta* classic, since we add a little thyme and turkey stock). The caramel flavors the ice cream and the skin gets folded into a magic brittle to preserve its crunch in sugary amber. No wonder people come into our shops to have an I-dare-you taste, then end up leaving with several scoops.

3 cups Ice Cream
   Base (page 34),
   very cold

³/₄ cup Salted Turkey
   Caramel (recipe
   follows), at room
   temperature

¹/₂ cup Turkey Skin
   Brittle (recipe
   follows)

Put the ice cream base, caramel, and ½ cup water into a bowl and whisk to combine. Pour the mixture into an ice cream maker and turn on the machine. Churn just until the mixture has the texture of soft-serve (see pages 23 to 24 for timing ranges, depending on the machine).

Quickly transfer the ice cream into freezer-friendly containers: Spoon in a layer of ice cream, sprinkle on some of the brittle, and use a spoon to press it in gently. Repeat. Cover with parchment paper, pressing it to the surface of the ice cream so it adheres, then cover with a lid. It's okay if the parchment hangs over the rim. Store it in the coldest part of your freezer (farthest from the door) until firm, at least 6 hours. It will keep for up to 3 months.

SALTED TURKEY CARAMEL

MAKES ABOUT 1½ CUPS

1 cup granulated
  sugar

¼ cup light corn
  syrup

½ cup heavy cream

1 cup turkey stock
  (store-bought
  is fine)

2 tablespoons turkey
  fat (rendered
  when you make the
  brittle, page 212;
  or use chicken fat)

2 teaspoons kosher
  salt

Pinch dried or
  generous pinch
  fresh thyme leaves

Combine the sugar, corn syrup, and ¼ cup water in a medium saucepan, and stir until all of the sugar looks wet. Cover the pan, set it over medium-high heat, and cook, stirring occasionally, until the sugar has completely melted, about 3 minutes.

Continue to cook, covered but without stirring, until the mixture has thickened slightly, about 3 minutes. Remove the lid and continue cooking, not stirring but paying close attention, until the mixture turns the color of very dark maple syrup and begins to smoke, 5 to 8 minutes more.

Take the pan off the heat, whisk the mixture, and continue whisking while you immediately pour in the cream (stand back!) and the turkey stock in a nice steady stream (whatever you do, do not dump it all in at once!). It'll bubble furiously.

Put the pot over medium-high heat again and attach a candy thermometer to the side. Let the mixture simmer away, stirring it occasionally, until it registers 230°F, 15 to 20 minutes. Take the pan off the heat and add the turkey fat, salt, and thyme, stirring slowly but constantly until the fat has completely melted.

Let the caramel cool to room temperature and transfer it to an airtight container. Store it at room temperature for up to 1 week. Separation is totally normal; just make sure to stir it well before using.

TURKEY SKIN BRITTLE

MAKES ABOUT 3 CUPS OF CHOPPED CANDY

½ cup big pieces of turkey (or chicken) skin (just stuff 'em into the measuring cup)

1 tablespoon vegetable oil

1 cup granulated sugar

½ cup light corn syrup

8 tablespoons (1 stick) unsalted butter

1 teaspoon kosher salt

1 teaspoon baking soda

Heat the oven to 350°F. Line a sheet pan with parchment paper.

Lightly coat the turkey skin with the vegetable oil and put the pieces on the lined sheet pan. Bake, rotating the pan halfway through, until they are richly browned and completely crispy, 15 to 30 minutes (turkey skin takes longer than chicken). Transfer the crisp skin to a cooling rack or a paper-towel-lined plate to cool to room temperature. Collect the rendered turkey fat from the sheet pan and reserve it for the caramel. Clean the sheet pan and line it with parchment again. Crumble the cooled turkey skin into ¼-inch or so pieces and use it within 2 hours.

Combine the sugar, corn syrup, and ½ cup water in a medium saucepan, and stir until all of the sugar looks wet. Set the pan over medium-high heat and cook, stirring occasionally, until the sugar has completely melted, about 3 minutes.

Continue to cook, this time covered and without stirring, until the mixture has thickened slightly, about 3 minutes. Add the butter and salt, then immediately stir until the butter has completely melted. Attach a candy thermometer to the side of the pan and let the mixture simmer away until it registers 290°F.

Remove the pan from the heat and quickly but thoroughly stir in the turkey skins, doing your best to distribute the pieces throughout the sticky mixture. Quickly and thoroughly stir in the baking soda (watch it all bubble!). Immediately pour the mixture onto the lined sheet pan, and quickly use a butter knife or a metal spatula to spread it out to a relatively even layer that's just under ¼ inch thick. Let the brittle sit uncovered until it has cooled to room temperature, about 1 hour.

Coarsely chop the brittle into small (no bigger than ¼-inch) pieces. Store them in an airtight container in the freezer until you are ready to use (or eat) them, up to 3 months. There's no need to defrost them before using.

PUMPKIN CUSTARD & SPICED GOAT CHEESE

MAKES ABOUT
2½
PINTS

If you're wise, you've ended many a Thanksgiving dinner with pumpkin pie topped with vanilla ice cream. I know I have, though I've always wished the sugar-on-sugar action had a little more balance. So after experimenting with many iterations of pumpkin ice cream, we decided to go a different, and I think more delicious, route. We swirled a silky-smooth custard—like liquid pumpkin pie filling!—into goat cheese ice cream, as tangy as it is sweet and infused with warming spices like allspice and nutmeg. Now you can end Thanksgiving dinner on a sophisticated note. Just kidding—you should definitely use this ice cream to top pumpkin pie!

1 large egg yolk

1 tablespoon granulated sugar

⅓ cup heavy cream

⅓ cup fresh goat cheese (I use chevre from Portland Creamery), at room temperature

1 teaspoon Pie Spices (recipe follows)

3 cups Ice Cream Base (page 34), very cold

1 teaspoon freshly squeezed lemon juice

1 cup Pumpkin Pie Custard (recipe follows)

In a large bowl, whisk the egg yolk and sugar together until the yolk begins to turn a lighter color. Heat the cream in a small saucepan over medium-high heat, stirring it constantly, until it is near a boil, about 1 minute. Very slowly drizzle the cream into the egg yolk, whisking constantly.

While the cream-egg mixture is still warm, add the goat cheese and pie spices and use a stick blender to incorporate them.

While the spiced goat cheese is still slightly warm, add the ice cream base and lemon juice, and blend thoroughly with the stick blender. Chill until cold.

Pour the mixture into an ice cream maker and turn on the machine. Churn just until it has the texture of soft-serve (see pages 23 to 24 for timing ranges, depending on the machine).

Alternate spooning layers of the ice cream and a dollop of the pumpkin pie custard in freezer-friendly containers.

Cover with parchment paper, pressing it to the surface of the ice cream so it adheres, then cover with a lid. It's okay if the parchment hangs over the rim. Store it in the coldest part of your freezer (farthest from the door) until firm, at least 6 hours. It will keep for up to 3 months.

PUMPKIN PIE CUSTARD

MAKES ABOUT 1½ CUPS

2 large egg yolks

½ cup granulated sugar

¼ cup light corn syrup

¾ cup Libby's pumpkin puree

1 teaspoon Pie Spices (recipe follows)

1 teaspoon vanilla extract

In a small saucepan, whisk together the egg yolks and sugar until the eggs turn a lighter color, about 1 minute. Add the corn syrup, pumpkin puree, pie spices, and vanilla and stir until completely combined. Cook the mixture over medium heat, stirring it constantly to prevent burning, until the custard has the consistency of pudding and turns a golden orange, 6 to 10 minutes. We're aiming for the color and mouthfeel of a standard pumpkin pie but with a slightly looser texture. It's important to cook this all the way through, both so that most of the water cooks off and so that the pumpkin gets a nice flavor.

Transfer to a container and cover the custard with plastic wrap directly on the surface so a skin doesn't form. Cool it in the fridge until it is cold to the touch before using it in the ice cream. Leftovers make a great pumpkin butter to slather on French toast . . . just sayin'.

PIE SPICES

MAKES ABOUT ¼ CUP

4 teaspoons ground cinnamon

2 teaspoons ground ginger

2 teaspoons kosher salt

1 teaspoon ground allspice

1 teaspoon ground nutmeg

1 teaspoon ground coriander

Put all the ingredients in a small bowl and whisk to combine. Store in an airtight container in a cool, dark place for up to 6 weeks.

CHAPTER 10

THE
HOLIDAY
SERIES

When we first launched a December holiday series, Kim and I had decided to enlist bartenders to share their creative winter cocktails, which I'd convert into scoopable form. (When you're an adult, the holiday season is fun but it also occasionally requires booze.) We were just about ready to greenlight the menu. But when we were seated around our pints, dipping in spoons to make a final assessment, we realized that while they all tasted different and exciting, the only pint the group had completely emptied was the one containing our straightforward take on eggnog. We had the same thought: I wish they were all like this eggnog.

You see, some traditions beg to be revamped—that's why our Thanksgiving series sets out to both please and provoke—but others deserve fidelity. That's why we decided to set invention aside and devote the Holiday collection to familiar flavors, just taken to new heights of tastiness. We double down on comfort and coziness and time-honored treats—gingerbread, chestnuts, hot cocoa with a peppermint stick for stirring—with a dash of ugly-Christmas-sweater camp.

PEPPERMINT COCOA
WITH HOMEMADE PEPPERMINT PATTIES

MAKES ABOUT
2½
PINTS

Imagine Santa sitting by the fire and stirring a steaming mug of hot cocoa with a peppermint stick, the astringent freshness infusing the cozy chocolate delight. Then picture him blowing out frosty breath, turning the whole thing cold and creamy. This is what happens in our version of that fantasy: folding in homemade peppermint patties that stud the cocoa scoop like Christmas lights. And even if you don't believe in Santa, you'll believe in magic when you taste what a few drops of peppermint oil can do.

¼ cup granulated sugar

¼ cup unsweetened cocoa powder (preferably Guittard's Cocoa Rouge)

1 drop peppermint oil (Seely Farm's peppermint oil is our favorite!)

3 cups Ice Cream Base (page 34), very cold

½ cup chopped Homemade Peppermint Patties (recipe follows)

Bring the sugar and ¼ cup water to a boil in a small saucepan and immediately take it off the heat, whisk in the cocoa powder, and keep at it until you have a smooth, sticky paste. Let it cool until it's just slightly warmer than room temperature. Add the peppermint oil and stir really well. Chill until cold; it will keep in an airtight container in the fridge for up to 3 days.

Put the cold peppermint-cocoa mixture and the ice cream base into a bowl and whisk to combine. Pour the mixture into an ice cream maker and turn on the machine. Churn just until the mixture has the texture of soft-serve (see pages 23 to 24 for timing ranges, depending on the machine).

Quickly transfer the ice cream into freezer-friendly containers: Spoon in a layer of ice cream, sprinkle on some of the peppermint patty pieces, and use a spoon to press them in gently. Repeat. Cover with parchment paper, pressing it to the surface of the ice cream so it adheres, then cover with a lid. It's okay if the parchment hangs over the rim. Store it in the coldest part of your freezer (farthest from the door) until firm, at least 6 hours. It will keep for up to 3 months.

HOMEMADE PEPPERMINT PATTIES

MAKES ABOUT 3 CUPS OF CHOPPED PIECES

½ cup semisweet
  chocolate chips

2 tablespoons
  unsalted butter

2 tablespoons
  evaporated milk

2 tablespoons light
  corn syrup

2 cups confectioners'
  sugar

2 drops peppermint
  oil (Seely's
  peppermint oil is
  our favorite!)

6 drops red or green
  food coloring
  (optional,
  depending on how
  festive you're
  feeling)

Line a sheet pan with parchment or wax paper.

Bring an inch or so of water to a simmer in a small saucepan. Put the chocolate chips in a heatproof bowl that will sit on the pan without touching the water. Set the bowl on the pan and heat the chocolate, stirring it occasionally, until it has completely melted. Take the pan off the heat but leave the bowl above the water so the chocolate stays melted.

Spoon about half of the chocolate onto the lined sheet pan. Use a regular or a pastry spatula to spread it out to form a round as thin as you can (about ¹⁄₁₆ inch thick). Let it cool until the chocolate has completely hardened, a few minutes.

In a separate small saucepan, combine the butter, evaporated milk, and corn syrup. Warm the mixture over low heat, stirring it occasionally, until it's warm to the touch and the butter is completely melted. Remove the pan from the heat and add about half of the confectioners' sugar. Stir with a sturdy spoon until smooth. Add the peppermint oil, food coloring (if using), and remaining confectioners' sugar and mix until you have a thick, smooth paste, about 3 minutes. Let it cool to room temperature.

You've got your cooled layer of chocolate. You've got your remaining melted chocolate. And you've got your peppermint paste. Now, you just assemble: Evenly spread the peppermint paste over the chocolate layer, smoothing out any peaks and valleys. Pour the remaining melted chocolate over the peppermint and spread it out in an even layer. Put the peppermint sandwich (still on the sheet pan) into the freezer and chill it for about 1 hour.

Cut the chilled sandwich into irregularly shaped bite-size (¼- to ½-inch) pieces. Use the candy immediately or save it in an airtight container in the freezer for up to 3 months.

GINGERBREAD COOKIE DOUGH

MAKES ABOUT
2½
PINTS

This flavor is a hug from Grandma Malek on Christmas morning. In each scoop, you'll find crumbles of Grandma's famous heavy-on-the-molasses gingerbread cookies and a little bit of holiday magic we call cookie butter (think peanut butter . . . but made out of cookies). And in a turn that's about as naughty as her secretly spiked eggnog, the vehicle for this cookie-powered festival of flavor is ice cream made in the style of hard sauce—the same glorious cold concoction of creamed butter, sugar, and rum that she used to dollop on her warm cookies.

In case you're wondering, no, you don't have to bake your own cookies for this flavor. Trust me, though, you'll be happy if you do. Not only does the aroma of gingerbread make for a happy household, but these particular cookies are designed to bake up especially tender so they don't freeze rock-hard.

3 cups Ice Cream Base (page 34), very cold

⅛ teaspoon kosher salt

⅛ teaspoon almond extract

⅛ teaspoon vanilla extract

1 teaspoon dark rum

1 cup Gingerbread "Cookie" pieces (recipe follows)

¾ cup Gingerbread Cookie Butter (recipe follows)

Put the ice cream base, salt, almond and vanilla extracts, and rum into a bowl and whisk to combine. Pour the mixture into an ice cream maker and turn on the machine. Churn just until the mixture has the texture of soft-serve (see pages 23 to 24 for timing ranges, depending on the machine).

Quickly transfer the ice cream into freezer-friendly containers: Spoon in layers of ice cream, sprinkles of the cookie pieces, using a spoon to press them in gently, and dollops of the cookie butter.

Cover with parchment paper, pressing it to the surface of the ice cream so it adheres, then cover with a lid. It's okay if the parchment hangs over the rim. Store it in the coldest part of your freezer (farthest from the door) until firm, at least 6 hours. It will keep for up to 3 months.

GINGERBREAD "COOKIES"

MAKES ABOUT 6 CUPS OF COOKIE PIECES

5 tablespoons
   unsalted butter,
   at room temperature

1/2 cup (lightly
   packed) light
   brown sugar

2 large eggs

2 tablespoons
   molasses (not
   blackstrap)

1 cup all-purpose
   flour

1/2 teaspoon baking
   soda

1/2 teaspoon ground
   cinnamon

1/8 teaspoon ground
   cloves

1/8 teaspoon ground
   ginger

1/8 teaspoon ground
   allspice

1/8 teaspoon kosher
   salt

Pinch freshly ground
   black pepper

While my grandma's cookies are such a pleasure when snatched off the countertop, they'd be rock-hard in a frozen scoop. To make a baked treat that eats like a cookie once it's embedded in ice cream, you must actually make cake, which means to make it a little lighter and puffier. That's why our snickerdoodles (see page 67) have extra leavening. So bake this easy gingerbread cake and don't tell Grandma Malek what we've done to her recipe.

Heat the oven to 350°F. Spray a standard-size loaf pan with nonstick cooking spray.

In a stand mixer fitted with the paddle attachment, or using a handheld mixer, cream the butter and brown sugar together by beating on medium speed until the mixture is slightly lighter in color and greater in volume. Add the eggs and molasses and mix on low speed until they are completely incorporated.

In a separate bowl, whisk together the flour, baking soda, cinnamon, cloves, ginger, allspice, salt, and pepper. Add the dry mixture to the wet one, and mix on medium-low speed just until combined.

Spread the batter out in the prepared loaf pan, forming an even layer all the way to the corners and edges. Bake until a toothpick inserted in the center comes out clean, about 30 minutes.

While it's still hot, invert the cake over a cooling rack to unmold it. Let it cool completely on the rack before using it. It will keep, covered, at room temperature for up to 1 week. Cut the gingerbread into ½-inch pieces before adding them to the ice cream.

GINGERBREAD COOKIE BUTTER

MAKES ABOUT ¾ CUP

$\frac{1}{2}$ cup Gingerbread
    "Cookie" pieces
    (opposite)

$\frac{1}{3}$ cup evaporated
    milk

1 tablespoon
    (lightly packed)
    light brown sugar

1 tablespoon
    unsalted butter,
    melted

$\frac{1}{2}$ teaspoon freshly
    squeezed lemon
    juice

In a food processor, pulse the gingerbread cookie pieces to the texture of fine bread crumbs. Add the evaporated milk, brown sugar, melted butter, and lemon juice, then process until smooth. Use the "butter" right away, or transfer it to an airtight container and store it in the fridge for up to 2 weeks.

APPLE BRANDY & PECAN PIE

MAKES ABOUT
2½
PINTS

You're somewhere in Oregon, sunk in a sofa near a fireplace after a day spent frolicking in fresh snow. You're sipping apple brandy, perhaps the pot-distilled marvel made by Clear Creek Distillery in Portland. Life is good. This is the cozy moment I wanted to channel with this flavor.

To make sure the brandy's amazingness wouldn't be obscured by sugar, fat, and freezing, I play up its fruity tartness with apple cider and its floralness (is that a word?) with vanilla. To make the ice cream bring to mind the velvety texture of the spirit, I decided on a custard base—that is, I added the lushness of eggs. And because in my cozy-on-the-sofa-with-brandy fantasy I'm eating pecan pie, I dreamed up—through many trials and many errors—tiny cubes of pecan pie that flaunt just the right amount of crumbly crust and soft filling, and stay that way even when frozen.

½ cup apple brandy

½ cup apple cider
  (or fresh apple
  juice)

½ cup whole milk

⅛ teaspoon ground
  cinnamon

¼ teaspoon kosher
  salt

¼ teaspoon
  vanilla extract,
  preferably Mexican

1 large egg yolk

3 cups Ice Cream
  Base (page 34),
  very cold

1 cup ½-inch cubes
  of Pecan Pie Bars
  (recipe follows)

In a small saucepan, combine the apple brandy and apple cider and cook over medium-high heat until they're reduced by half, to about ½ cup. Remove the pan from the heat and whisk in the milk, cinnamon, salt, vanilla, and egg yolk.

Put the pan back over medium heat and cook, stirring constantly, until the custard thickens just enough to coat the back of a spoon, about 8 minutes. Remove it from the heat, chill until cold, and use immediately or store in the fridge for up to 1 week. Whisk before using.

Put the ice cream base and the apple brandy custard into a bowl and whisk to combine. Pour the mixture into an ice cream maker and turn on the machine. Churn just until the mixture has the texture of soft-serve (see pages 23 to 24 for timing ranges, depending on the machine).

Quickly transfer the ice cream into freezer-friendly containers: Spoon in a layer of ice cream, sprinkle on some of the pecan pie bar bits, and use a spoon to press them in gently. Repeat. Cover with parchment paper, pressing it to the surface of the ice cream so it adheres, then cover with a lid. It's okay if the parchment hangs over the rim. Store it in the coldest part of your freezer (farthest from the door) until firm, at least 6 hours. It will keep for up to 3 months.

PECAN PIE BARS

MAKES 24 BARS

FOR THE CRUST

1 cup all-purpose
flour

1/4 cup granulated
sugar

1/8 teaspoon kosher
salt

8 tablespoons
(1 stick) cold
unsalted butter,
cut into 1/2-inch
cubes

FOR THE FILLING

1 cup granulated
sugar

3 tablespoons all-
purpose flour

1/2 teaspoon kosher
salt

1 cup dark corn
syrup

3 tablespoons
unsalted butter,
melted

1 tablespoon
molasses (not
blackstrap)

3 large eggs

1/2 teaspoon vanilla
extract

1 cup pecans,
chopped

MAKE THE CRUST

Heat the oven to 350°F. Spray a 9 × 13-inch sheet pan with nonstick cooking spray.

In a stand mixer fitted with the paddle attachment, combine the flour, sugar and salt. Add the butter and mix on medium speed just until the mixture looks like buttery pebbles. Dump the mixture onto the prepared sheet pan and use your hands to spread it out to cover the surface. Then use your hands to lightly press it to form an even layer. Bake until the dough is light brown on the top, 15 to 20 minutes.

Keep the oven on and let the crust hang out at room temperature while you make the filling.

MAKE THE FILLING

Combine the sugar, flour, and salt in the clean bowl of the stand mixer fitted with the whisk attachment and mix well. Add the corn syrup, melted butter, molasses, eggs, and vanilla, and mix on medium-low speed until smooth.

Sprinkle the pecans over the baked crust, then pour the filling mixture over the nuts in an even layer. Bake until the pecan filling is set around the edges and slightly jiggly in the middle, about 25 minutes. Let it cool and then cut it into whatever size bars you like. The bars will keep in an airtight container in the fridge for up to 1 week.

BUTTER-ROASTED CHESTNUT

If your only experience with chestnuts roasting comes from "The Christmas Song," you're missing out. When intense heat licks the shells of chestnuts, a rich, sweet smell fills the air and all is right with the world. That's the feeling you'll get with each spoonful once you roast your own and blend them with brown butter and sea salt to make an ice cream smoother than Nat King Cole's baritone.

6 ounces chestnuts in their shells (or 3 ounces vacuum-sealed peeled chestnuts— see Note)

2 cups plus 2 tablespoons hot water

3 tablespoons unsalted butter

3 tablespoons really great dark local honey

1¼ teaspoons fleur de sel

3 cups Ice Cream Base (page 34), very cold

Heat the oven to 425°F.

Using a sharp knife, carefully cut a large "X" through the shell on the bottom of each chestnut. Each cut should be about ¾ inch across and just deep enough to go through the shell.

If using nuts in their shells, put the chestnuts in a bowl, cover with the 2 cups hot water, and let sit for 5 to 10 minutes so that they absorb some water, then drain them (this will help them steam once in the oven and their shells will peel off much more easily).

Put the nuts on a sheet pan and roast them in the oven for 30 to 45 minutes; the shells will curl upward where they've been cut, and the exposed flesh should be as tender as a fully baked potato when you poke it with a paring knife. Let the chestnuts sit until they are just cool enough to handle, and peel them while they are still warm. Put the peeled, still-warm chestnuts in a food processor, add the remaining 2 tablespoons hot water, and let them sit.

Melt the butter in a small saucepan over medium heat and cook, stirring it often with a spatula to prevent the solids from burning, until it turns a medium amber and smells nutty, 3 to 5 minutes. Remove the pan from the heat and add the honey and fleur de sel. Whisk until smooth.

Add the butter mixture to the chestnuts in the food processor and puree until smooth, about 3 minutes. Cool to room temperature. Keep the chestnut butter in the food processor if you're using it right away, or store it in an airtight container in the fridge for up to 1 week. (Gently warm it to room temperature before using.)

(recipe continues)

NOTE

*If you're using
vacuum-packed peeled
chestnuts, skip the
soaking and roasting,
and put them directly
in the food processor
with the hot water.*

Pour the ice cream base into the processor with the chestnut mixture and briefly process until well mixed. If using a frozen-bowl machine, transfer the mixture to a container and chill, covered, until cold. Pour the mixture into an ice cream maker and turn on the machine. Churn just until the mixture has the texture of soft-serve (see pages 23 to 24 for timing ranges, depending on the machine).

Transfer the ice cream, scraping every last delicious drop from the machine, into freezer-friendly containers. Cover with parchment paper, pressing it to the surface of the ice cream so it adheres, then cover with a lid. It's okay if the parchment hangs over the rim. Store it in the coldest part of your freezer (farthest from the door) until firm, at least 6 hours. It will keep for up to 3 months.

FENNEL FIVE-SPICE EGGNOG

MAKES ABOUT

2½

PINTS

Poor, poor eggnog, whose reputation has been ruined by the contents of cartons. The shake-and-pour supermarket stuff bears no relation to the simple, elegant cocktail of brandy and cream invented long ago. When I engineered this velvet pudding-on-a-spoon, we decided to make it family-friendly, so I skipped the alcohol and used Chinese five spice to replace the warming complexity that booze typically provides, boosting the fennel seed component with the magic dust also known as fennel pollen.

This recipe makes a little extra eggnog mixture. Add a bit of half-and-half and drink it—now would be a great time to add that brandy.

1½ cups whole milk

¼ cup honey

¼ teaspoon fennel pollen (optional, but strongly recommended)

¼ teaspoon fennel seeds

One 2-inch cinnamon stick, lightly crushed

1 black peppercorn, lightly crushed

1 tea bag black tea

⅛ teaspoon ground cardamom

One 4 × ¾-inch strip orange zest

½ teaspoon kosher salt

½ teaspoon vanilla extract

2 large egg yolks

⅛ teaspoon freshly grated nutmeg

3 cups Ice Cream Base (page 34), very cold

Line a fine-mesh strainer with cheesecloth or a coffee filter.

In a small saucepan, combine the milk, honey, fennel pollen (if using), fennel seeds, cinnamon stick, peppercorn, tea bag, cardamom, orange zest, and salt. Set the pan over medium heat and cook, stirring occasionally, until the mixture is hot to the touch. Remove the pan from the heat and let the mixture steep for 5 minutes. Then strain it through the lined strainer into a container, discard the solids, and return the strained mixture to the saucepan.

Whisk in the vanilla, egg yolks, and nutmeg. Put the pan back over medium heat and cook, whisking constantly, until the mixture thickens enough to coat the back of a spoon, about 3 minutes. Remove it from the heat, let it cool completely, and refrigerate in an airtight container until cold; it will keep for up to 1 week. Whisk before using.

Put the ice cream base and 1 cup of the eggnog mixture into a bowl and whisk to combine. Pour the mixture into an ice cream maker and turn on the machine. Churn just until the mixture has the texture of soft-serve (see pages 23 to 24 for timing ranges, depending on the machine).

Transfer the ice cream, scraping every last delicious drop from the machine, into freezer-friendly containers. Cover with parchment paper, pressing it to the surface of the ice cream so it adheres, then cover with a lid. It's okay if the parchment hangs over the rim. Store it in the coldest part of your freezer (farthest from the door) until firm, at least 6 hours. It will keep for up to 3 months.

ACKNOWLEDGMENTS

To my cousin, friend, and business partner, Kim Malek, who designed this company so thoughtfully and has led it in such a way that it makes the people and community around her better.

To our Salt & Straw team: To Casey, who if you ask me is the most talented hospitality-focused mind of our generation and whose genius is to make food culture approach-able. If you're ever lucky enough to talk with her, she might change your life. To Kat, James, Kristen, Rudy, Amanda, Ian, Laura, and David, some of the first people we ever hired and still leaders in our company. We're all here (five hundred "Salties" and count-ing!) because we believe ice cream has the ability to change the world. I'm honored and grateful that you have given so much time and energy and life force to help make this company what it is. To the rest of our lead-ership team: Austin Ketchum, Kavita Patel, and Nicki Kerbs; to Melissa Broussard, our amazing publicist; and to Kathleen Healy, our invaluable real estate broker.

To Mike Axley, Kim's partner, who not even a year into their relationship put up his house as collateral to help us start this company—and who let me move into his basement! To Sandy Ryan, Kim's sister-in-law, who came up with our name and has given me tons of fun flavor "ideas" ever since.

To my wife, Sophia, you are everything to me. You push me to be smarter and more thoughtful. You will be fighting by my side till the end of the world. To my grandmas—Grandma Malek, who I learned how to cook from, and Grandma Joan, who I learned how to cook for. To my grandpas—Grandpa Malek, who offered endless support, and Grandpa Norm, who inspired me to do and try every-thing so I could be anything. To my mom and dad, who loved and supported me through every step. And to my stepdad, who, when he was slowly slipping away, fighting off cancer, was the first person to genuinely *love* some-thing I cooked. You are one big reason I'm in a kitchen today.

To Francis Lam and JJ Goode, who are the reason this book was written. Francis met with Kim and me when we were just a tiny company in Portland and convinced us we had a story that needed to be told. That conversation, one of the deepest and real-est we'd had then or since, has guided a lot of the ways in which we took our business. Then, after spending two years sitting on scribbled notes and drawings, JJ is the one who swooped in to help get things off the ground, forcing me to stick to deadlines and, in tandem with Francis, helping in every way imaginable to get this finished. These two are my heroes.

To Andrew Thomas Lee, who shut himself in a tiny room with me for, like, two hundred hours to take these photos. The only prompt we started with was to "do something with ice cream that's never been done before," and dang, he killed it. To Andrea Slonecker, Caroline Wright, and Emily Stephenson, who were by my side the entire way, testing the recipes to ensure they worked perfectly in a home kitchen. And to Andee Hess, one of the best designers in the country, who has lent her genius to Salt & Straw's aesthetic since 2013 and is one reason this book looks so beautiful.

To the design team at Clarkson Potter, Jen Wang and Stephanie Huntwork, who patiently, skillfully, and diligently worked to help me execute my vision for this book. And to the production team of Chris Tanigawa and Heather Williamson, who made it real.

To Kim Witherspoon and her team at Inkwell Management for helping to get the project off the ground.

To Danny Meyer, Peter Mavrovitis, Mark Leavitt, and the rest of the Enlightened Hospitality Investment team, as well as Billy Logan, Alan Karp, and the KarpReilly team. You believed in us early and have been 110 percent supportive of our vision for a company that invests back in their people and communities.

To the cities—L.A., San Francisco, San Diego, Seattle—that have welcomed us with open arms. And to the city of Portland, where we got our start, that supported us through it all. To everyone who waited in line for a lick, and to the chefs, artists, artisans, and citizens whose generosity and collaborative spirit inspires me every day. Just to name a few: Mark Bitterman, David Briggs, Gabe Rucker, Gregory Gourdet, Jenn Louis, Gaby and Greg Denton, Charley Wheelock, Ben Jacobsen, Tom McMahon, Steven Smith, Tony Tellin, Michael Madigan, Sarah Masoni, Geoff Latham, the team at OP, the team at Feast PDX, Red Ridge Farms, Congressman Earl Blumenauer, Karen Brooks, and Thomas Lauderdale.

INDEX

Published in the United States by Clarkson Potter/
Publishers, an imprint of the Crown Publishing
Group, a division of Penguin Random House LLC,
New York.
crownpublishing.com
clarksonpotter.com

CLARKSON POTTER is a trademark and POTTER
with colophon is a registered trademark
of Penguin Random House LLC.

Library of Congress Cataloging-in-Publication Data
is available upon request.

ISBN 978-1-5247-6015-1
Ebook ISBN 978-1-5247-6016-8

Printed in China

Book and cover design by Jen Wang
Photographs by Andrew Thomas Lee
Art on page 176 by Rudy Speerschneider

10 9 8 7 6 5 4 3

First Edition